Data Mining and Warehousing: Clustering and Outlier Mining Approach

Dr.R. Prabahari,

Assistant Professor,

PG & Research Department of Computer Science,

Gobi Arts & Science College, Gobichettipalayam.

Dr.V. Thiagarasu,

Associate Professor,

PG & Research Department of Computer Science,

Gobi Arts & Science College, Gobichettipalayam.

Dr.M. Ramalingam,

Assistant Professor,

PG & Research Department of Computer Science,

Gobi Arts & Science College, Gobichettipalayam.

Published by

Data Mining and Warehousing: Clustering and Outlier Mining Approach

Copyright © 2018 by Bonfring

All rights reserved. Authorized reprint of the edition published by Bonfring. No part of this book may be reproduced in any form without the written permission of the publisher.

Limits of Liability/Disclaimer of Warranty: The authors are solely responsible for the contents of the paper in this volume. The publishers or editors do not take any responsibility for the same in any manner. Errors, if any, are purely unintentional and readers are required to communicate such errors to the editors or publishers to avoid discrepancies in future. No warranty may be created or extended by sales or promotional materials. The advice and strategies contained herein may not be suitable for every situation. This work is sold with the understanding that the publisher is not engaged in rendering legal, accounting, or other professional services. If professional assistance is required, the services of a competent professional person should be sought. Further, reader should be aware that internet website listed in this work may have changed or disappeared between when this was written and when it is read.

Bonfring also publishes its books in a variety of electronic formats. Some content that appears in print may not be available in electronic books.

ISBN 978-93-86638-75-5

Authors

Dr.R. Prabahari

Dr.V. Thiagarasu

Dr.M. Ramalingam

Bonfring

309, 2nd Floor, 5th Street Extension, Gandhipuram,

Coimbatore-641 012.

Tamilnadu, India.

E-mail: info@bonfring.org

Website: www.bonfring.org

Phone: 0422 4213231

Preface

"Give a man a fish and he'll eat for a day. Teach him to fish and he'll eat forever"

-A Chinese proverb

In today's world raw data is being collected by companies at an exploding rate. For example, Walmart processes over 20 million point-of-sale transactions every day. This information is stored in a centralized database, but would be useless without some type of data mining software to analyze it. If Walmart analyzed their point-of-sale data with data mining techniques they would be able to determine sales trends, develop marketing campaigns and more accurately predict customer loyalty.

"What we have is a data glut." – Vernor Vinge, emeritus professor of mathematics at San Diego State University, who is considered of the greatest science fiction writers today.

"The goal is to turn data into information and information into insight." – **Carly Fiorina,** former executive, president and chair of Hewlett-Packard Co.

"You can have data without information, but you cannot have information without data."– **Daniel Keys Moran**, an American computer programmer and science fiction writer.

"When we have all data online it will be great for humanity. It is a prerequisite to solving many problems that humankind faces." – **Robert Cailliau,** Belgian informatics engineer and computer scientist who, together with Tim Berners-Lee, developed the World Wide Web.

Data mining can help spot sales trends, develop smarter marketing campaigns and accurately predict customer loyalty. Data mining is a process used by companies to turn raw data into useful information. By using software to look for patterns in large batches of data, businesses can learn more about their customers and develop more effective marketing strategies as well as increase sales and decrease costs. In the study of human genetics, sequence mining helps address the important goal of understanding the mapping relationship between the inter-individual variations in human DNA sequence and the variability in disease susceptibility. In simple terms, it aims to find out how the changes in an individual's DNA sequence affects the risks of developing common diseases such as cancer, which is of great importance to improve methods of diagnosing, preventing and treating these diseases. In recent times, that has seen a tremendous growth in the field of biology such as genomics, proteomics, functional Genomics and biomedical research. Biological data mining is a very important part of Bioinformatics. Data mining concepts are still evolving and here are the latest trends that get to see in this book.

Dr.R. Prabahari

Dr.V. Thiagarasu

Dr.M. Ramalingam

Acknowledgement

We would like to submit our deep sense of gratitude to the Management, Gobi Arts & Science College (Autonomous) for providing us an opportunity to publish the book.

We would like to express our heart-felt gratitude and sincere thanks to the Principal Prof. Dr.R. Sellappan, Gobi Arts & Science College (Autonomous), Gobichettipalayam for bringing out this book.

It gives us an immense debt of gratitude to express our sincere thanks to Prof. P. Narendran, Head & Associate Professor of Computer Science, Gobi Arts & Science College (Autonomous), Gobichettipalayam for the support towards their book.

We extend my sincere thanks to all the staff members, PG & Research Department of Computer Science, Gobi Arts & Science College (Autonomous), Gobichettipalayam for the moral support towards our book work and useful suggestions rendered by them. We are also thankful to the publishers for bringing out the book fruitfully.

Completion of this book could not have been accomplished without the support of our family and friends. We would like to extend our special thanks to whole family and our friends.

Dr.R. Prabahari
Dr.V. Thiagarasu
Dr.M. Ramalingam

About the Authors

Dr.R. Prabahari, is an Assistant Professor in the Department of Computer Science, Gobi Arts & Science College, Gobichettipalayam. She has 11 years of experience in teaching. She has published more than 10 papers in international journals and conferences. Her Research focuses on outlier mining for discovering abnormal and irregular patterns of images efficiently, by improving cluster quality. She is a Life Member in Indian Science Congress.

Dr.V. Thiagarasu is an Associate Professor in the Department of Computer Science, Gobi Arts & Science College, Gobichettipalayam. He has more than two and half decades experience in teaching and research. He has handled projects funded by UGC and has published more than 50 papers in reputed international journals and conferences. His research areas include Data Mining, Networks. He is a Life Member in various professional bodies such as Indian Science Congress, Operational Research Society of India, Computer Society of India and Senior Member in International Association of Computer Science & Information Technology and Member in International Association of Engineers.

Dr.M. Ramalingam is an Assistant Professor in the Department of Computer Science, Gobi Arts & Science College, Gobichettipalayam. He has 4 years of relevant industrial experience and decade of rich experience in research and teaching. He has published more than 25 papers in international journals and conferences. His Research focuses on Cluster based Mobile Ad hoc Network and MANET security. He is a Life Member in Indian Science Congress, Computer Science Teachers Association (CSTA), Society of Digital Information and Wireless Communications (SDIWC), Internet Society (ISOC) and Member in The Global Community of Information Professionals.

<table>
<tr><th>Chapter</th><th>Contents</th><th>Page No</th></tr>
</table>

CHAPTER I

DATA MINING AND DATA WAREHOUSING

1.1. Knowledge Discovery in Database

KDD refers to the overall process of discovering useful knowledge from data. It involves the evaluation and possibly interpretation of the patterns to make the decision of what qualifies as knowledge. It also includes the choice of encoding schemes, preprocessing, sampling, and projections of the data prior to the data mining step.

Across a wide variety of fields, data are being collected and accumulated at a dramatic pace. There is an urgent need for a new generation of computational theories and tools to assist humans in extracting useful information (knowledge) from the rapidly growing volume of digital data. These theories and tools are the subject of the emerging field of Knowledge Discovery in Database (KDD). At an abstract level, the KDD field is concerned with the development of methods and techniques for making sense of data. The basic problem addressed by the KDD process is the mapping of low level data (which are typically too voluminous to understand and digest easily) into other forms that might be more compact (short report), more abstract (descriptive approximation or model of the process that generated the data), or more useful (predictive model for estimating the value of future cases) [Frawley W.J et al., 1991].

KDD is the non-trivial process of identifying valid, novel, potentially useful and ultimately understandable patterns in data [Fayyad et al., 1996]. Data are a set of facts and pattern is an expression in some language describing a subset of the data or a model applicable to the subset. Extracting a pattern also designates fitting a model to data, finding structure from data or in general, making any high level description of a set of data. The term process implies that KDD comprises many steps, which involve data preparation, search for patterns and knowledge evaluation. By non-trivial means that search or inference is involved, it is not a straight forward computation of pre-defined quantities like computing the average value of a set of numbers. The discovered patterns should be valid on new data with a certain degree of certainty and potentially useful, lead to some benefit to the user or task. Finally, the patterns should be understandable, if not immediately after the post-processing. Data mining is a step in the KDD process that consists of applying data analysis and discovery algorithms, under acceptable computational efficiency limitations; produce a particular enumeration of patterns (or models) over the data.

The KDD process is using the database along with any required selection, pre-processing, sub-sampling and transformations of it; applying data mining methods (algorithms) to enumerate patterns from it; evaluating the products of data mining to identify the subset of the enumerated patterns deemed knowledge. The data mining component of the KDD process is concerned with the algorithmic means by which patterns are extracted and enumerated from data [Ester M et al., 1996]. Historically, the notion of finding useful patterns in data have been given a variety of names including data mining, knowledge extraction, information discovery, information harvesting, data archaeology and data pattern processing. The term data mining has mostly been used by statisticians, data analysts and the Management Information Systems (MIS) communities. It has also gained popularity in the database field. KDD refers to the overall process of discovering useful knowledge from data and data mining refers to a particular step in this process. Data mining is the application of specific algorithms for extracting patterns from data. The additional steps in the KDD process such as data preparation, data selection, data cleaning and incorporation of appropriate prior knowledge and proper interpretation of the results of mining are essential to ensure that useful knowledge is derived from the data. Blind application of data mining methods can be a dangerous activity, easily leading to the discovery of meaningless and invalid patterns.

The KDD process can be viewed as a multi disciplinary activity that encompasses techniques beyond the scope of any one particular discipline. In this context, there are clear opportunities for other fields of AI (besides machine learning) to contribute to KDD. KDD places a special emphasis on finding understandable patterns that can be interpreted as useful or interesting knowledge. Thus, for example neural networks, although a powerful modeling tools are relatively difficult to understand compared to decision trees. KDD also emphasizes scaling and robustness properties of modeling algorithms for large noisy datasets. Knowledge discovery from data is fundamentally a statistical endeavor.

Database techniques for gaining efficient data access, grouping and ordering operations when accessing data and optimizing queries constitute the basics for scaling algorithms to larger data sets. Most data mining algorithms from statistics, pattern recognition and machine learning assume data are in the main memory and pay no attention to the algorithm breaks down if only limited views of the data are possible. A related field evolving from database is data warehousing which refers to the popular business trend of collecting and cleaning transactional data to make them available for online analysis and decision support [Frawley et al., 1991]. Data warehousing helps for KDD in two important ways [Fayyad U. M, 2001]: (1) Data cleaning and (2) Data access.

Data Cleaning: As organizations are forced to think about a unified logical view of the wide variety of data and databases they possess, to address the issues of mapping data to a single naming convention, uniformly representing and handling missing data and handling noise and errors when possible.

Data Access: Uniform and well defined methods must be created for accessing the data and providing access paths to data that were historically difficult to get (for example stored offline). Once organizations and individuals have solved the problem of store and access the data. A popular approach for analysis of data warehouse is called OnLine Analytical Processing (OLAP). OLAP tools focus on providing multidimensional data analysis, which is superior to Structured Query Language (SQL) in computing summaries and breakdowns along many dimensions. OLAP tools are targeted toward simplifying and supporting interactive data analysis but the goal of KDD tools is to automate as much of the process as possible. Thus, KDD is a step beyond currently supported by most standard database systems.

1.2. Basic Steps of the KDD Process

- **Data Cleaning** – the noise and inconsistent data is removed.
- **Data Integration** – multiple data sources are combined.
- **Data Selection** – data relevant to the analysis task are retrieved from the database.
- **Data Transformation** – data is transformed or consolidated into forms appropriate for mining by performing summary or aggregation operations.
- **Data Mining** – intelligent methods are applied in order to extract data patterns.
- **Pattern Evaluation** – data patterns are evaluated.
- **Knowledge Presentation** – knowledge is represented.

The KDD process is interactive and iterative, involving numerous steps with many decisions made by the user and it is in nine basic steps [Frawley et al., 1991].

- **Developing:** An understanding of the application domain and the relevant prior knowledge and identifying the goal of the KDD process from the customer's view point.
- **Target data set:** Selecting a data set or focusing on a subset of variables or data samples on which discovery is to be performed.
- **Cleaning and pre-processing:** Basic operations include removing noise if appropriate, collecting the necessary information to model or account for noise, deciding on strategies for handling missing data fields and accounting for time sequence information and known changes.

- **Data reduction and projection:** Finding useful features to represent the data depending on the goal of the task. With dimensionality reduction or transformation methods, the effective number of variables under consideration can be reduced or invariant representations for the data can be found.

- **Matching:** The goals of the KDD process to a particular data mining method for example summarization, classification, regression, clustering and so on.

- **Exploratory analysis:** Choosing the data mining algorithm(s) and selecting method(s) to be used for searching for data patterns. This process includes deciding which models and parameters might be appropriate and matching a particular data mining method with the overall criteria of the KDD process.

- **Data mining:** Searching for patterns of interest in a particular representational form or a set of such representations including classification rules or trees, regression and clustering. The user can significantly aid the data mining method by correctly performing the preceding steps.

- **Interpreting mined patterns:** Possibly returning to any of steps one through seven for further iteration. This step can also involve visualization of the extracted patterns and models or visualization of the data given the extracted models.

- **Discovered knowledge:** Using the knowledge directly, incorporating the knowledge into another system for further action or simply documenting it and reporting it to the interested parties [Frawley et al., 1991].

1.2.1. *Elements of KDD*

Pattern: Any representation formalism capable to describe the common characteristics of a group if instances.

Valid: A pattern is valid if it is able to predict the behavior of new information with a degree of certainty.

Novelty: It is novel any knowledge that it is not know respect the domain knowledge and any previous discovered knowledge.

Useful: New knowledge is useful if it allows performing actions that yield some benefit given established criteria.

Understandable: The knowledge discovered must be analyzed by an expert in the domain in consequence the interpretability of the result is important.

1.2.2. Goals of the KDD Process

Classification: Discriminate instances that belong to a previously known set of groups

Clustering/Partitioning/Segmentation: Discover models that clusters the data into groups with common characteristics

Regression: Predicts the behaviour of continuous variables as a function of others

Summarization: Summarizes the characteristics of the data.

Causal dependence: Causal dependence among the variables and assess the strength of this dependence.

Structure dependence: Relations that describe the structure of the data.

Change: Discover patterns in data that has temporal or spatial dependence.

1.2.3. Methodologies for KDD

There are a lot of methodologies that can be applied in the discovery process, the more usual are:

Decision Trees, Decision Rules

Usually are interpretable models

Can be used for: Classification, regression, and summarization

Trees: C4.5, CART, QUEST

 rules: RIPPER, CN2 .

Classifiers, Regression: Low interpretability but good accuracy.

Can be used for: Classification and regression Statistical regression, function approximation, Neural networks, Support Vector Machines, k-NN, Local Weighted Regression.

Clustering: Its goal is to partition datasets or discover groups

Can be used for: Clustering, summarization Statistical Clustering, Unsupervised Machine learning, Unsupervised Neural networks (Self-Organizing Maps)

Dependency models: Its goal is to obtain models of the dependence relations among attributes/instances

Can be used for: causal dependence discovery, temporal change, substructure discovery Bayesian networks, association rules, Markov models, graph algorithms.

1.2.4. Applications

Business: Costumer segmentation, costumer profiling, costumer transaction data, customer churn Fraud detection Control/analysis of industrial processes e-commerce, on-line recommendation Financial data.

WEB mining: Text mining, document search/organization, Social networks analysis, User behaviour.

Scientific applications: Medicine (patient data, MRI scans, ECG, EEG,) Pharmacology (Drug discovery, screening, in-silicon testing) Astronomy (astronomical bodies identification) Genetics (gen identification, DNA microarrays, bioinformatics) Satellite/Probe data (meteorology, astronomy, geological) Large scientific experiments (CERN LHC, ITER).

Data mining sometimes called data or knowledge discovery. It is the process of analyzing data from different perspectives and summarizing it into useful information. Data mining software is one of a number of analytical tools for analyzing data. It allows users to analyze data from many different dimensions or angles, categorize it, and summarize the relationships identified. Technically, data mining is the process of finding correlations or patterns among dozens of fields in large relational databases. Data mining refers to extracting or "mining" knowledge from large amounts of data. The term is actually a misnomer. Remember that the mining of gold from rocks or sand is referred to as gold mining rather than rock or sand mining. Thus, data mining should have been more appropriately named "knowledge mining from data," which is unfortunately somewhat long. "Knowledge mining," a shorter term may not reflect the emphasis on mining from large amounts of data. Nevertheless, mining is a vivid term characterizing the process that finds a small set of precious nuggets from a great deal of raw material. Thus, such a misnomer that carries both "data" and "mining" became a popular choice. Many other terms carry a similar or slightly different meaning to data mining, such as knowledge mining from data, knowledge extraction, data/pattern analysis, data archaeology, and data dredging. Many people treat data mining as a synonym for another popularly used term, Knowledge Discovery from Data, or KDD. Alternatively, others view data mining as simply an essential step in the process of knowledge discovery.

1.3. Data Mining

Data mining is a step in the KDD process of applying data analysis and discovery algorithms under acceptable computational efficiency limitations, produce a particular enumeration of patterns (or models) on the data. With the enormous amount of data stored in files, databases and other repositories, it is increasingly important, necessary to develop powerful means for analysis and perhaps interpretation of such data and for the extraction of interesting knowledge that could help in decision making. Data mining and Knowledge Discovery in Databases (or KDD) are frequently treated as synonyms data mining is actually part of the knowledge discovery process.

Data mining is an iterative process within which progress is defined by discovery, through either automatic or manual methods. Data mining is most useful in an exploratory analysis scenario in which there are no pre-determined notions about what will constitute an "interesting" outcome. Data mining is search for the new, valuable and non-trivial information in large volumes of data. It is a cooperative effort of humans and computers. Best results are achieved by balancing the knowledge of human experts in describing problems and goals with the search capabilities of computers. In practice, the two primary goals of data mining tend to be prediction and description [Chen M. S et al., 1996]. Prediction involves using some variables or fields in the data set to predict unknown or future values of other variables of interest. Description, on the other hand, focuses on finding patterns are describing the data that can be interpreted by humans. Therefore, it is possible to put data mining activities into one of two categories:

- Predictive data mining, this produces the model of the system described by the given data set.
- Descriptive data mining, which produces new, non-trivial information based on the available data set.

On the predictive end of the goal of data mining is to produce a model, expressed as an executable code, which can be used to perform classification, prediction, estimation or other similar tasks. On the other hand, descriptive, end of the goal is to gain an understanding of the analyzed system by uncovering patterns and relationships in large data sets [Kumar V, 2011].

1.3.1. *Data Mining Tasks [Chen M.S et al., 1996]*

- **Classification** - Discovery of a predictive learning function that classifies a data item into one of several predefined classes.
- **Regression** - Discovery of a predictive learning function, which maps a data item to a real value prediction variable.
- **Clustering** - A common descriptive task in which one seeks to identify a finite set of categories or clusters to describe the data.
- **Summarization** - An additional descriptive task that involves methods for finding a compact description for a set (or subset) of data.

- **Dependency Modeling**-Finding a local model that describes significant dependencies between variables or between the values of a feature in a data set or in a part of a data set.

- **Change and Deviation Detection** [Bakar Z et al., 2006]-Discovering the most significant changes in the data set.

The demand of data mining is growing increasingly fast for extracting useful information from a data set. The theory of data mining becomes more and more significant. Data mining is the exploration and analysis of large data sets, in order to discover meaningful pattern and rules [Hand D et al., 2001]. The key idea is to be found effective way to combine the computer's power to process the data with the human eye's ability to detect patterns. Data mining applications are financial data analysis, telecommunication industries, retail industries, health care and biomedical research and science and engineering.

The objective of data mining is designed for large and it is the component of wider process called knowledge discovery from database [Han J and Kamber M, 2001]. Mining of data is done through data pre-processing, various models and complexity considerations, inference considerations, post-processing of that pre-processed data, visualization and finally updating. The data, which is accessed, can be stored in one or more operational databases. The data is mined using two learning approaches are supervised learning and unsupervised learning [Han J and Kamber M, 2001].

1.3.2. Supervised Learning

The supervised learning also called directed data mining, the variables under investigation can be split into two groups, explanatory variables and one or more dependent variables. The goal of the analysis is to specify a relationship between the dependent variable and explanatory variables as it is done in regression analysis. To proceed with directed data mining techniques the values of the dependent variable must be known for a sufficiently large part of the data set. Supervised learning is the machine learning task of inferring a function from labeled training data. The training data consist of a set of training examples. In supervised learning, each example is a pair consisting of an input object (typically a vector) and a desired output value (also called the supervisory signal). A supervised learning analysis the training data and produces an inferred function, which can be used for mapping new examples. An optimal scenario will allow for the algorithm to correctly determine the class labels for unseen instances. This requires the learning algorithm to generalize from the training data to unseen situations in a "reasonable" way.

In order to solve a given problem of supervised learning has to perform the following steps:

- Determine the type of training examples. Before doing anything else, the user should decide the kind of data is to be used as a training set. In the case of handwriting analysis, for example, this might be a single handwritten character, an entire handwritten word or an entire line of handwriting.

- Determine the training set. The training set needs to be representative of the real world use of the function. Thus, a set of input objects is gathered and corresponding outputs are also gathered either from human experts or from measurements.

- Determine the input feature representation of the learned function. The accuracy of the learned function depends strongly on the input object is represented. Typically, the input object is transformed into a feature vector, which contains a number of features that are descriptive of the object. The number of features should not be too large, because of the dimensionality but should contain enough information to accurately predict the output.

- Determine the structure of the learned function and corresponding learning algorithm. For example, the engineer may choose to use support vector machines or decision trees.

- Complete the design. Run the learning algorithm on the gathered training set. Some supervised learning algorithms require the user to determine certain control parameters. These parameters may be adjusted by optimizing performance on a subset (called a validation set) of the training set or via cross validation.

- Evaluate the accuracy of the learned function. After parameter adjustment and learning, the performance of the resulting function should be measured on a test set that is separate from the training set.

Given a set of n training examples of the form $\{(x1, y1)... (xn , yn)\}$. Such that $x_i 1$ is the feature vector of the ith example and $y_i 1$ is its label (i.e., class), a learning algorithm seeks a function $g: x \rightarrow y$, where x is the input space and y is the output space [Han D et al., 2001].

The function g is an element of some space of possible functions G, usually called the hypothesis space.

It is sometimes convenient to represent g using a scoring function $f: x * y \rightarrow R$ such that g is defined as returning the y value that gives the highest score:

$$g(x) = arg\_max \, f(x,y).$$

Let f denote the space of scoring functions. Although g and f can be any space of functions, many learning algorithms are probabilistic models where g takes the form of a conditional probability model $g(x) = p(y/x)$, or f takes the form of a joint probability model $f(x,y) = p(x$

,y). For example, Naive Bayes and linear discriminate analysis are joint probability models, whereas logistic regression is a conditional probability model.

There are two basic approaches to choosing f or g: empirical risk minimization and structural risk minimization. Empirical risk minimization seeks the function that best fits the training data. Structural risk minimize includes a penalty function that controls the bias/variance tradeoffs.

In both cases, it is assumed that the training set consists of a sample of independent and identically distributed pairs, (x_i, y_i). In order to measure a function fits the training data, a loss function $L: Y * Y \rightarrow R >= 0$ is defined. For training example (x_i, y_i), the loss of predicting the value $\hat{y}$ is $L(y_i, \hat{y})$.

The risk $R(g)$ of function g is defined as the expected loss of g. This can be estimated from the training data as

$$R_{emp}(g) = 1/N \sum L(y_i, g(x_i)).$$

Empirical Risk Minimization

In empirical risk minimization, the supervised learning algorithm seeks the function g that minimizes $R(g)$. Hence, a supervised learning algorithm can be constructed by applying an optimization algorithm to find g. When g is a conditional probability distribution $p(y/x)$ and the loss function is the negative log likelihood: $L(y, \hat{y}) = -\log P(y/x)$, then empirical risk minimization is equivalent to maximum likelihood estimation. When G contains many candidate functions or the training set is not sufficiently large, empirical risk minimization leads to high variance and poor generalization. The learning algorithm is able to memorize the training examples without generalizing well. This is called over fitting.

Structural Risk Minimization

Structural risk minimization seeks to prevent over fitting by incorporating a regularization penalty into the optimization. The regularization penalty can be viewed as implementing a form of Occam's razor that prefers simpler functions over more complex ones.

A wide variety of penalties have been employed that correspond to different definitions of complexity. For example, consider the case where the function g is a linear function of the form.

$$g(x) = \sum_{j=1}^{n} \beta^2_j x_j$$

A popular regularization penalty is $\sum \beta^2_j$, which is the squared Euclidean norm of the weights, also known as the L_2 norm. Other norms include the L_1 norm, $\sum \beta^2_j$, and the L_0 norm, which is the number of non-zero β_j s. The penalty will be denoted by C (g). The supervised learning optimization problem is to find the function g that minimizes

$$J(g) = R_{emp}(g) + \lambda C(g)$$

The parameter λ controls the bias-variance tradeoffs. When $\lambda=0$, this gives empirical risk minimization with low bias and high variance. When λ is large, the learning algorithm will have high bias and low variance. The value of λ can be chosen empirically via cross validation. The complexity penalty has a Bayesian interpretation as the negative log prior probability of g, -logP (g), in which case J(g) is the posterior probability of g.

Generative Training

The training methods described above are discriminative training methods, because they seek to find a function g that discriminates well between the different output values. For the special case where f(x,y)=P(x,y) is a joint probability distribution and the loss function is the negative log likelihood $-\sum logP(x_i,y_i)$ a risk minimization algorithm is said to perform generative training, because f can be regarded as a generative model that explains how the data were generated. Generative training algorithms are often simpler and more computationally efficient than discriminative training algorithms. In some cases, the solution can be computed in closed form as in naive Bayes and linear discriminant analysis.

Generalizations of Supervised Learning

There are several ways in which the standard supervised learning problem can be generalized:

- **Semi supervised learning**: In this setting, the desired output values are provided only for a subset of the training data. The remaining data is unlabeled.
- **Active learning:** Instead of assuming that all of the training examples are given at the start, active learning algorithms interactively collect new examples, typically by making queries to a human user. Often, the queries are based on unlabeled data, which is a scenario that combines semi-supervised learning with active learning.
- **Structured prediction:** When the desired output value is a complex object, such as a parse tree or labeled graph then standard methods must be extended.
- **Learning to rank:** When the input is a set of objects and the desired output is a ranking of those objects then again the standard methods must be extended.

A wide range of supervised learning algorithms is available, each with its strengths and weaknesses. There is no single learning algorithm that works as the best on all supervised learning problems.

In Table 1.1 describes a supervised learning, a basket filled with some different kinds of fruits, the task is to arrange the fruit as groups. First, find the names of the fruits in the basket and then types of fruits. There are apple, banana, grape and cherry already learnt from the previous work about the physical characters of fruits. So arranging the same type of fruits at one place is easy now. The previous work is called as training data in data mining and already learns the things from training data; this is because of response variable. Response variable mean just a decision variable. In Table 1.1 shows observe response variable below (fruit name).

Table 1.1: Supervised Learning

S. No.	Size	Color	Decision variable	Fruit name
1	Big	Red	Rounded shape with a depression at the top	Apple
2	Small	Red	Heart-shaped to nearly globular	Cherry
3	Big	Green	Long curving cylinder	Banana
4	Small	Green	Round to oval, Bunch shape Cylindrical	Grape

Suppose taken a new fruit from the basket then the size, color and shape of that particular fruit. If size is Big, color is Red, shape is rounded shape with a depression at the top, conform the fruit name as apple and put in apple group. Likewise, for other fruits also. Learn the thing before from training data and then applying that knowledge to the test data (for new fruit). This type of learning is called as supervised learning. Classification comes under supervised learning.

1.3.3. Unsupervised Learning

In unsupervised learning, all the variables are treated in same way; there is no distinction between dependent and explanatory variables. However, in contrast to the name undirected data mining still there is some target to achieve. This target might be as data reduction as general or more specific like clustering. The dividing line between unsupervised learning and supervised learning is the same that distinguishes discriminate analysis from cluster analysis [Kejia Zhang et al., 2007]. Supervised learning requires target variable should be well defined and that a sufficient number of its values are given. Unsupervised learning typically either the target variable has only been recorded for too small a number of cases or the target variable is unknown [Kejia Zhang et al., 2007].

The tasks of data mining are very diverse and distinct because there are many patterns in large data set. Different types of methods and techniques are needed to find different kinds of pattern.

Based on kinds of pattern, tasks in data mining can be classified into Anomaly detection, Association rule, Classification, Regression, Summarization and Clustering analysis.

- **Anomaly detection (Outlier/change/deviation detection)** [Ghosh A.K et al., 1998]: The identification of unusual data records that might be data errors that require further investigation.

- **Association rule learning (Dependency modeling):** Searches for relationships between variables.

- **Clustering** [Yasmanishi K and Ichi Takeuchi, 2001]: It is the task of discovering groups and structures in the data that are in some way or another "similar", without using known structures in the data.

- **Classification:** It is the task of generalizing known structure to apply to new data. For example, an e-mail program attempts to classify an e-mail as "legitimate" or as "spam".

- **Regression:** Attempts to find a function which models the data with the least error.

- **Summarization:** Providing a more compact representation of the data set, this includes visualization and report generation.

A good clustering method produces high quality clusters with high intra cluster similarity and low inters cluster similarity. The quality of a result produced by clustering depends on both the similarity measure used by the method and its implementation. The quality of a clusters produced by clustering method is also measured by its ability to discover some or all of the hidden patterns. The requirements of clustering algorithms are scalability, ability to deal with insensitivity to the order of input records and with noisy data.

1.4.   Major Components of Data Mining System

Database, data warehouse, World Wide Web, or other information repository: This is one or a set of databases, data warehouses, spreadsheets, or other kinds of information repositories. Data cleaning and data integration techniques may be performed on the data.

Database or data warehouse server: The database or data warehouse server is responsible for fetching the relevant data, based on the user's data mining request.

Knowledge base: This is the domain knowledge that is used to guide the search or evaluate the interestingness of resulting patterns. Such knowledge can include concept hierarchies, used to organize attributes or attribute values into different levels of abstraction. Knowledge such as user beliefs, which can be used to assess a pattern's interestingness based on its unexpectedness, may also be included. Other examples of domain knowledge are additional interestingness constraints or thresholds, and metadata.

Data mining engine: This is essential to the data mining system and ideally consists of a set of functional modules for tasks such as characterization, association and correlation analysis, classification, prediction, cluster analysis, outlier analysis, and evolution analysis.

Pattern evaluation module: This component typically employs interestingness measures and interacts with the data mining modules so as to focus the search toward interesting patterns. It may use interestingness thresholds to filter out discovered patterns. Alternatively, the pattern evaluation module may be integrated with the mining module, depending on the implementation of the data mining method used. For efficient data mining, it is highly recommended to push the evaluation of pattern interestingness as deep as possible into the mining process so as to confine the search to only the interesting patterns.

User interface: This module communicates between users and the data mining system, allowing the user to interact with the system by specifying a data mining query or task, providing information to help focus the search, and performing exploratory data mining based on the intermediate data mining results. In addition, this component allows the user to browse database and data warehouse schemas or data structures, evaluate mined patterns, and visualize the patterns in different forms.

Data mining involves an integration of techniques from multiple disciplines such as database and data warehouse technology, statistics, machine learning, high-performance computing, pattern recognition, neural networks, data visualization, information retrieval, image and signal processing, and spatial or temporal data analysis. For an algorithm to be scalable, its running time should grow approximately linearly in proportion to the size of the data, given the available system resources such as main memory and disk space. By performing data mining, interesting knowledge, regularities, or high-level information can be extracted from databases and viewed or browsed from different angles. The discovered knowledge can be applied to decision making, process control, information management, and query processing. Therefore, data mining is considered one of the most important frontiers in database and information systems and one of the most promising interdisciplinary developments in the information technology.

1.5. Data Mining Algorithms and Techniques

Various algorithms and techniques like Classification, Clustering, Prediction, Association Rules, Neural Networks etc., are used for knowledge discovery from databases.

1.5.1. *Classification*

Classification is the most commonly applied data mining technique, which employs a set of pre-classified examples to develop a model that can classify the population of records at large. Fraud detection and credit risk applications are particularly well suited to this type of analysis. This approach frequently employs decision tree or neural network-based classification algorithms. The data classification process involves learning and classification. In Learning the training data are analyzed by classification algorithm. In classification test data are used to estimate the accuracy of the classification rules. If the accuracy is acceptable the rules can be applied to the new data tuples. For a fraud detection application, this would include complete records of both fraudulent and valid activities determined on a record-by-record basis. The classifier-training algorithm uses these pre-classified examples to determine the set of parameters required for proper discrimination. The algorithm then encodes these parameters into a model called a classifier.

Types of classification models:

- Classification by decision tree induction
- Bayesian Classification
- Neural Networks
- Support Vector Machines (SVM)
- Classification Based on Associations

1.5.2. *Clustering*

Clustering can be said as identification of similar classes of objects. By using clustering techniques to identify dense and sparse regions in object space and can discover overall distribution pattern and correlations among data attributes. Classification approach can also be used for effective means of distinguishing groups or classes of object but it becomes costly so clustering can be used as preprocessing approach for attribute subset selection and classification.

For example, to form group of customers based on purchasing patterns, to categories genes with similar functionality.

Types of clustering methods

- Partitioning Methods
- Hierarchical Agglomerative (divisive) methods
- Density based methods
- Grid-based methods
- Model-based methods

1.5.3. *Predication*

Regression technique can be adapted for predication. Regression analysis can be used to model the relationship between one or more independent variables and dependent variables. In data mining independent variables are attributes already known and response variables are wanted to predict. Unfortunately, many real-world problems are not simply prediction. For instance, sales volumes, stock prices, and product failure rates are all very difficult to predict because they may depend on complex interactions of multiple predictor variables. Therefore, more complex techniques may be necessary to forecast future values. The same model types can often be used for both regression and classification. For example, the CART (Classification and Regression Trees) decision tree algorithm can be used to build both classification trees and regression trees. Neural networks too can create both classification and regression models.

Types of regression methods

Linear Regression

- Multivariate Linear Regression
- Nonlinear Regression
- Multivariate Nonlinear Regression

1.5.4. *Association Rule*

Association and correlation is usually to find frequent item set findings among large data sets. This type of finding helps businesses to make certain decisions, such as catalogue design, cross marketing and customer shopping behavior analysis.

Association Rule algorithms need to be able to generate rules with confidence values less than one. However the number of possible Association Rules for a given dataset is generally very large and a high proportion of the rules are usually of little (if any) value.

Types of association rule

- Multilevel association rule
- Multidimensional association rule
- Quantitative association rule

1.5.5. Neural Networks

Neural network is a set of connected input/output units and each connection has a weight present with it. During the learning phase, network learns by adjusting weights so as to be able to predict the correct class labels of the input tuples. Neural networks have the remarkable ability to derive meaning from complicated or imprecise data and can be used to extract patterns and detect trends that are too complex to be noticed by either humans or other computer techniques. These are well suited for continuous valued inputs and outputs. For example handwritten character reorganization, for training a computer to pronounce English text and many real world business problems and have already been successfully applied in many industries. Neural networks are best at identifying patterns or trends in data and well suited for prediction or forecasting needs.

Types of neural networks

- Back Propagation

1.6. Applications of Data Mining

Data mining applications are used in various fields.

Healthcare

Data mining holds great potential to improve health systems. It uses data and analytics to identify best practices that improve care and reduce costs. Researchers use data mining approaches like multi-dimensional databases, machine learning, soft computing, data visualization and statistics. Mining can be used to predict the volume of patients in every category. Processes are developed that make sure that the patients receive appropriate care at the right place and at the right time. Data mining can also help healthcare insurers to detect fraud and abuse.

Market Basket Analysis

Market basket analysis is a modelling technique based upon a theory that if buy a certain group of items are more likely to buy another group of items. This technique may allow the retailer to understand the purchase behaviour of a buyer. This information may help the retailer to know the buyer's needs and change the store's layout accordingly. Using differential analysis comparison of results between different stores, between customers in different demographic groups can be done.

Education

There is a new emerging field, called Educational Data Mining, concerns with developing methods that discover knowledge from data originating from educational Environments. The goals of EDM are identified as predicting students' future learning behaviour, studying the effects of educational support, and advancing scientific knowledge about learning. Data mining can be used by an institution to take accurate decisions and also to predict the results of the student. With the results the institution can focus on what to teach and how to teach. Learning pattern of the students can be captured and used to develop techniques to teach them.

Manufacturing Engineering

Knowledge is the best asset a manufacturing enterprise would possess. Data mining tools can be very useful to discover patterns in complex manufacturing process. Data mining can be used in system-level designing to extract the relationships between product architecture, product portfolio, and customer needs data. It can also be used to predict the product development span time, cost, and dependencies among other tasks.

CRM

Customer Relationship Management is all about acquiring and retaining customers, also improving customers' loyalty and implementing customer focused strategies. To maintain a proper relationship with a customer a business need to collect data and analyse the information. This is where data mining plays its part. With data mining technologies the collected data can be used for analysis. Instead of being confused where to focus to retain customer, the seekers for the solution get filtered results.

Fraud Detection

Billions of dollars have been lost to the action of frauds. Traditional methods of fraud detection are time consuming and complex. Data mining aids in providing meaningful patterns and turning data into information. Any information that is valid and useful is knowledge. A perfect fraud detection system should protect information of all the users. A supervised method includes collection of sample records. These records are classified fraudulent or non-fraudulent. A model is built using this data and the algorithm is made to identify whether the record is fraudulent or not.

Intrusion Detection

Any action that will compromise the integrity and confidentiality of a resource is an intrusion. The defensive measures to avoid an intrusion includes user authentication, avoid programming errors, and information protection. Data mining can help improve intrusion detection by adding a level of focus to anomaly detection. It helps an analyst to distinguish an activity from common everyday network activity. Data mining also helps extract data which is more relevant to the problem.

Lie Detection

Apprehending a criminal is easy whereas bringing out the truth from him is difficult. Law enforcement can use mining techniques to investigate crimes, monitor communication of suspected terrorists. This filed includes text mining also. This process seeks to find meaningful patterns in data which is usually unstructured text. The data sample collected from previous investigations is compared and a model for lie detection is created. With this model processes can be created according to the necessity.

Customer Segmentation

Traditional market research may help us to segment customers but data mining goes in deep and increases market effectiveness. Data mining aids in aligning the customers into a distinct segment and can tailor the needs according to the customers. Market is always about retaining the customers. Data mining allows finding a segment of customers based on vulnerability and the business could offer them with special offers and enhance satisfaction.

Financial Banking

With computerised banking everywhere huge amount of data is supposed to be generated with new transactions. Data mining can contribute to solving business problems in banking and finance by finding patterns, causalities, and correlations in business information and market prices that are not immediately apparent to managers because the volume data is too large or is generated too quickly to screen by experts. The managers may find this information for better segmenting, targeting, acquiring, retaining and maintaining a profitable customer.

Corporate Surveillance

Corporate surveillance is the monitoring of a person or group's behaviour by a corporation. The data collected is most often used for marketing purposes or sold to other corporations, but is also regularly shared with government agencies. It can be used by the business to tailor their products desirable by their customers.

The data can be used for direct marketing purposes, such as the targeted advertisements on Google and Yahoo, where ads are targeted to the user of the search engine by analyzing their search history and emails.

Research Analysis

History shows that witnessed revolutionary changes in research. Data mining is helpful in data cleaning, data pre-processing and integration of databases. The researchers can find any similar data from the database that might bring any change in the research. Identification of any co-occurring sequences and the correlation between any activities can be known. Data visualisation and visual data mining provide us with a clear view of the data.

Criminal Investigation

Criminology is a process that aims to identify crime characteristics. Actually crime analysis includes exploring and detecting crimes and their relationships with criminals. The high volume of crime datasets and also the complexity of relationships between these kinds of data have made criminology an appropriate field for applying data mining techniques. Text based crime reports can be converted into word processing files. This information can be used to perform crime matching process.

Bio Informatics

Data Mining approaches seem ideally suited for Bioinformatics, since it is data-rich. Mining biological data helps to extract useful knowledge from massive datasets gathered in biology, and in other related life sciences areas such as medicine and neuroscience. Applications of data mining to bioinformatics include gene finding, protein function inference, disease diagnosis, disease prognosis, disease treatment optimization, protein and gene interaction network reconstruction, data cleansing, and protein sub-cellular location prediction.

Service Providers

Mining and Business Intelligence comes from service providers in the mobile phone and utilities industries. Mobile phone and utilities companies use Data Mining and Business Intelligence to predict 'churn', the terms they use for when a customer leaves their company to get their phone/gas/broadband from another provider. They collate billing information, customer services interactions, website visits and other metrics to give each customer a probability score, then target offers and incentives to customers whom they perceive to be at a higher risk of churning.

Retail

Another example of Data Mining and Business Intelligence comes from the retail sector. Retailers segment customers into 'Regency, Frequency, Monetary' (RFM) groups and target marketing and promotions to those different groups. A customer who spends little but often and last did so recently will be handled differently to a customer who spent big but only once, and also some time ago. The former may receive a loyalty, upsell and cross-sell offers, whereas the latter may be offered a win-back deal, for instance.

E-commerce

Perhaps some of the most well -known examples of Data Mining and Analytics come from E-commerce sites. Many E-commerce companies use Data Mining and Business Intelligence to offer cross-sells and up-sells through their websites. One of the most famous of these is, of course, Amazon, who use sophisticated mining techniques to drive their, 'People who viewed that product, also liked this' functionality.

Supermarkets

Supermarkets provide another good example of Data Mining and Business Intelligence in action. Famously, supermarket loyalty card programmes are usually driven mostly, if not solely, by the desire to gather comprehensive data about customers for use in data mining. One notable recent example of this was with the US retailer Target. As part of its Data Mining programme, the company developed rules to predict if their shoppers were likely to be pregnant. By looking at the contents of their customers' shopping baskets, they could spot customers who they thought were likely to be expecting and begin targeting promotions for nappies (diapers), cotton wool and so on. The prediction was so accurate that Target made the news by sending promotional coupons to families who did not yet realise (or who had not yet announced) they were pregnant!

Crime Agencies

The use of Data Mining and Business Intelligence is not solely reserved for corporate applications and this is shown in the final example. Beyond corporate applications, crime prevention agencies use analytics and Data Mining to spot trends across myriads of data – helping with everything from where to deploy police manpower (where is crime most likely to happen and when?), who to search at a border crossing (based on age/type of vehicle, number/age of occupants, border crossing history) and even which intelligence to take seriously in counter-terrorism activities.

1.7. Data Warehouse Architectures

The following architecture properties are essential for a data warehouse system (Kelly, 1997):

- **Separation:** Analytical and transactional processing should be kept apart as much as possible.
- **Scalability:** Hardware and software architectures should be easy to upgrade as the data volume, which has to be managed and processed, and the number of users' requirements, which have to be met, progressively increase.
- **Extensibility:** The architecture should be able to host new applications and technologies without redesigning the whole system.
- **Security Monitoring:** Accesses is essential because of the strategic data stored in data warehouses.
- **Administer ability:** Data warehouse management should not be overly difficult.

1.7.1. Single-Layer Architecture

Single-layer architecture is not frequently used in practice. Its goal is to minimize the amount of data stored; to reach this goal, it removes data redundancies. Fig 1.1 shows the only layer physically available: the source layer. In this case, data warehouses are virtual.

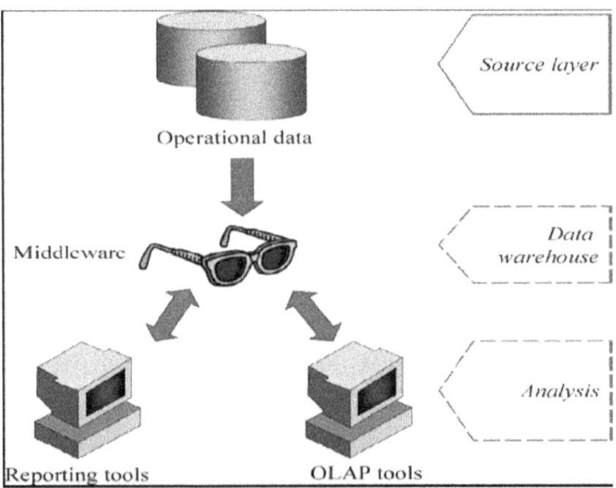

Fig. 1.1: Single-layer Architecture for a Data Warehouse System

This means that a data warehouse is implemented as a multidimensional view of operational data created by specific middleware, or an intermediate processing layer (Devlin, 1997).

The weakness of this architecture lies in its failure to meet the requirement for separation between analytical and transactional processing. Analysis queries are submitted to operational data after the middleware interprets them. It this way, the queries affect regular transactional workloads. In addition, although this architecture can meet the requirement for integration and correctness of data, it cannot log more data than sources do. For these reasons, a virtual approach to data warehouses can be successful only if analysis needs are particularly restricted and the data volume to analyze is huge.

1.7.2. Two-Layer Architecture

The requirement for separation plays a fundamental role in defining the typical architecture for a data warehouse system, as shown in Fig 1-2. Although it is typically called two-layer architecture to highlight a separation between physically available sources and data warehouses, it actually consists of four subsequent data flow stages (Lechtenbörger, 2001):

- **Source layer**: data warehouse system uses heterogeneous sources of data. That data is originally stored to corporate relational databases or legacy1 databases, or it may come from information systems outside the corporate walls.

- **Data staging:** The data stored to sources should be extracted, cleansed to remove inconsistencies and fill gaps, and integrated to merge heterogeneous sources into one common schema. The so-called Extraction, Transformation, and Loading tools (ETL) can merge heterogeneous schemata, extract, transform, cleanse, validate, filter, and load source data into a data warehouse (Jarke et al., 2000). Technologically speaking, this stage deals with problems that are typical for distributed information systems, such as inconsistent data management and incompatible data structures (Zhuge et al., 1996).

- **Data warehouse layer:** Information is stored to one logically centralized single repository: a data warehouse. The data warehouse can be directly accessed, but it can also be used as a source for creating data marts, which partially replicate data warehouse contents and are designed for specific enterprise departments. Meta-data repositories store information on sources, access procedures, data staging, users, data mart schemata, and so on.

- **Analysis:** In this layer, integrated data is efficiently and flexibly accessed to issue reports, dynamically analyze information, and simulate hypothetical business scenarios. Technologically speaking, it should feature aggregate data navigators, complex query optimizers, and user-friendly GUIs.

The architectural difference between data warehouses and data marts needs to be studied closer. The component marked as a data warehouse in Fig 1.2 is also often called the primary data warehouse or corporate data warehouse. It acts as a centralized storage system.

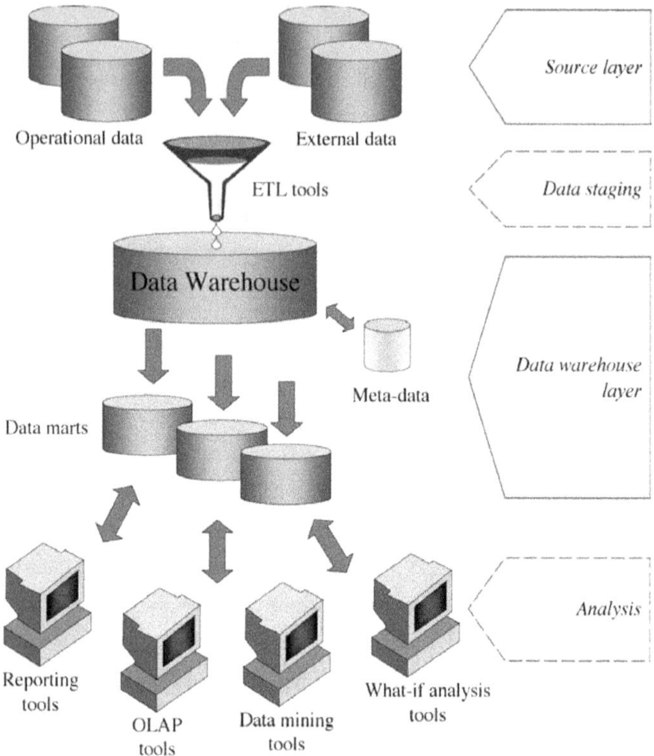

Fig. 1.2: Two-layer Architecture for a Data Warehouse System

All the data being summed up. Data marts can be viewed as small, local data warehouses replicating (and summing up as much as possible) the part of a primary data warehouse required for a specific application domain.

The data marts populated from a primary data warehouse are often called dependent. Although data marts are not strictly necessary, they are very useful for data warehouse systems in midsize to large enterprises because

- Used as building blocks while incrementally developing data warehouses;
- Mark out the information required by a specific group of users to solve queries;
- Deliver better performance because they are smaller than primary data warehouses.

Sometimes, mainly for organization and policy purposes, should use a different architecture in which sources are used to directly populate data marts. These data marts are called independent. If there is no primary data warehouse, this streamlines the design process, but it leads to the risk of inconsistencies between data marts. To avoid these problems, it can create a primary data warehouse and still have independent data marts. In comparison with the standard two-layer architecture of Figure 1-3, the roles of data marts and data warehouses are actually inverted. In this case, the data warehouse is populated from its data marts, and it can be directly queried to make access patterns as easy as possible.

The following list sums up all the benefits of a two-layer architecture, in which a data warehouse separates sources from analysis applications (Jarke et al., 2000; Lechtenbörger, 2001):

- In data warehouse systems, good quality information is always available, even when access to sources is denied temporarily for technical or organizational reasons.
- Data warehouse analysis queries do not affect the management of transactions, the reliability of which is vital for enterprises to work properly at an operational level.
- Data warehouses are logically structured according to the multidimensional model, while operational sources are generally based on relational or semi-structured models.
- A mismatch in terms of time and granularity occurs between OLTP systems, which manage current data at a maximum level of detail, and OLAP systems, which manage historical and summarized data.
- Data warehouses can use specific design solutions aimed at performance optimization of analysis and report applications.

1.7.3. Three-Layer Architecture

In this architecture, the third layer is the reconciled data layer or operational data store. This layer materializes operational data obtained after integrating and cleansing source data. As a result, those data are integrated, consistent, correct, current, and detailed. Fig 1.3 shows a data warehouse that is not populated from its sources directly, but from reconciled data.

The main advantage of the reconciled data layer is that it creates a common reference data model for a whole enterprise. At the same time, it sharply separates the problems of source data extraction and integration from those of data warehouse population. Remarkably, in some cases, the reconciled layer is also directly used to better accomplish some operational tasks, such as producing daily reports that cannot be satisfactorily prepared using the corporate applications, or generating data flows to feed external processes periodically so as to benefit from cleaning and integration. However, reconciled data leads to more redundancy of operational source data. Note, may assume that even two-layer architectures can have a reconciled layer that is not specifically materialized, but only virtual, because it is defined as a consistent integrated view of operational source data.

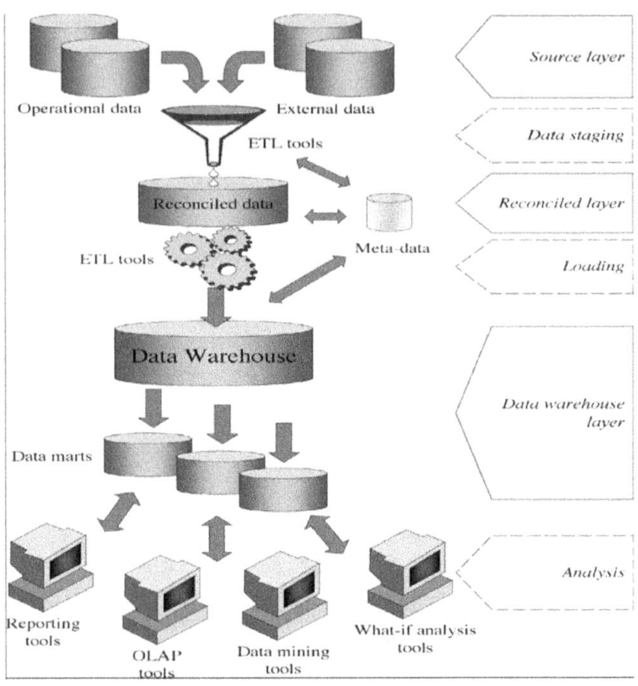

Fig. 1.3: Three-layer Architecture for a Data Warehouse System

Finally, let's consider a supplementary architectural approach, which provides a comprehensive picture. This approach can be described as a hybrid solution between the single-layer architecture and the two/three-layer architecture. This approach assumes that although a data warehouse is available, it is unable to solve all the queries formulated. This means that users may be interested in directly accessing source data from aggregate data (drill-through). To reach this goal, some queries have to be rewritten on the basis of source data (or reconciled data if it is available). This type of architecture is implemented in a prototype by Cui and Widom, 2000, and it needs to be able to go dynamically back to the source data required for queries to be solved (lineage).

1.7.4. An Additional Architecture Classification

The scientific literature often distinguishes five types of architecture for data warehouse systems, in which the same basic layers mentioned in the preceding paragraphs are combined in different ways (Rizzi, 2008).

In independent data marts architecture, different data marts are separately designed and built in a nonintegrated fashion. This architecture can be initially adopted in the absence of a strong sponsorship toward an enterprise-wide warehousing project, or when the organizational divisions that make up the company are loosely coupled. However, it tends to be soon replaced by other architectures that better achieve data integration and cross-reporting.

The bus architecture, recommended by Ralph Kimball, is apparently similar to the preceding architecture, with one important difference. A basic set of conformed dimensions (that is, analysis dimensions that preserve the same meaning throughout all the facts they belong to), derived by a careful analysis of the main enterprise processes, is adopted and shared as a common design guideline. This ensures logical integration of data marts and an enterprise-wide view of information.

In the hub-and-spoke architecture, one of the most used in medium to large contexts, there is much attention to scalability and extensibility, and to achieving an enterprise-wide view of information.

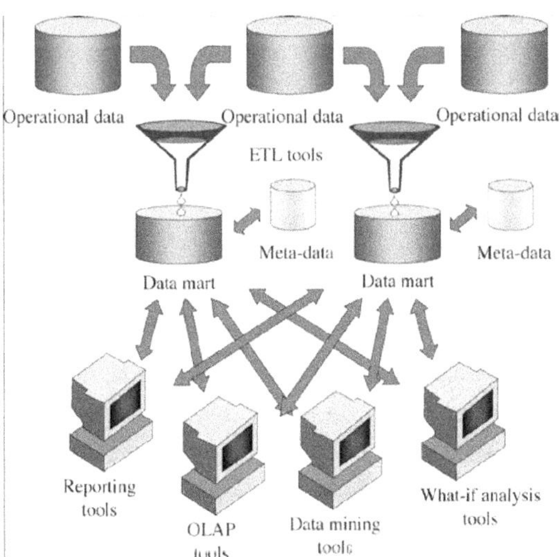

Fig. 1.4: Independent Data Marts Architecture

Atomic, normalized data is stored in a reconciled layer that feeds a set of data marts containing summarized data in multidimensional form. Users mainly access the data marts, but they may occasionally query the reconciled layer. The centralized architecture, recommended by Bill Inmon, can be seen as a particular implementation of the hub-and-spoke architecture, where the reconciled layer and the data marts are collapsed into a single physical repository.

The federated architecture is sometimes adopted in dynamic contexts where preexisting data warehouses/data marts are to be noninvasively integrated to provide a single, cross-organization decision support environment (for instance, in the case of mergers and acquisitions). Each data warehouse/data mart is either virtually or physically integrated with the others, leaning on a variety of advanced techniques such as distributed querying, ontologies, and meta-data interoperability. The following list includes the factors that are particularly influential when it comes to choosing one of these architectures:

- The amount of interdependent information exchanged between organizational units in an enterprise and the organizational role played by the data warehouse project sponsor may lead to the implementation of enterprise-wide architectures, such as bus architectures, or department-specific architectures, such as independent data marts.

- An urgent need for a data warehouse project, restrictions on economic and human resources, as well as poor IT staff skills may suggest that a type of "quick" architecture, such as independent data marts, should be implemented.

- The minor role played by a data warehouse project in enterprise strategies can make the prefer an architecture type based on independent data marts over a hub-and-spoke architecture type.

- The frequent need for integrating preexisting data warehouses, possibly deployed on heterogeneous platforms, and the pressing demand for uniformly accessing their data can require a federated architecture type.

1.8. Data Staging and ETL

Now let's closely study some basic features of the different architecture layers. Start with the data staging layer. The data staging layer hosts the ETL processes that extract, integrate, and clean data from operational sources to feed the data warehouse layer. In three-layer architecture, ETL processes actually feed the reconciled data layer—a single, detailed, comprehensive, top-quality data source-that in its turn feeds the data warehouse. For this reason, the ETL process operations as a whole are often defined as reconciliation. These are also the most complex and technically challenging among all the data warehouse process phases.

ETL takes place once when a data warehouse is populated for the first time, then it occurs every time the data warehouse is regularly updated. ETL consists of four separate phases: extraction (or capture), cleansing (or cleaning or scrubbing), transformation, and loading.

The scientific literature shows that the boundaries between cleansing and transforming are often blurred from the terminological viewpoint. For this reason, a specific operation is not always clearly assigned to one of these phases. This is obviously a formal problem, but not a substantial one. It will adopt the approach used by Hoffer and others (2005) to make explanations as clear as possible. Their approach states that cleansing is essentially aimed at rectifying data values, and transformation more specifically manages data formats.

Extraction: Relevant data is obtained from sources in the extraction phase. It can use static extraction when a data warehouse needs populating for the first time. Conceptually speaking, this looks like a snapshot of operational data. Incremental extraction, used to update data warehouses regularly, seizes the changes applied to source data since the latest extraction. Incremental extraction is often based on the log maintained by the operational DBMS. If a timestamp is associated with operational data to record exactly when the data is changed or added, it can be used to streamline the extraction process. Extraction can also be source-driven if rewrite operational applications to asynchronously notify of the changes being applied, or if your operational database can implement triggers associated with change transactions for relevant data. The data to be extracted is mainly selected on the basis of its quality. In particular, this depends on how comprehensive and accurate the constraints implemented in sources are, how suitable the data formats are, and how clear the schemata are.

1.9. Multidimensional Model

The data warehouse layer is a vitally important part of this book. Here, introduce a data warehouse key word: multidimensional. Its need to become familiar with the concepts and terminology used here to understand the information presented throughout this book, particularly information regarding conceptual and logical modeling and designing.

Over the last few years, multidimensional databases have generated much research and market interest because they are fundamental for many decision-making support applications, such as data warehouse systems. The reason why the multidimensional model is used as a paradigm of data warehouse data representation is fundamentally connected to its ease of use and intuitiveness even for IT newbies.

The multidimensional model's success is also linked to the widespread use of productivity tools, such as spreadsheets, that adopt the multidimensional model as a visualization paradigm.

Perhaps the best starting point to approach the multidimensional model effectively is a definition of the types of queries for which this model is best suited.

- "What is the total amount of receipts recorded last year per state and per product category?"
- "What is the relationship between the trend of PC manufacturers' shares and quarter gains over the last five years?"
- "Which orders maximize receipts?"
- "Which one of two new treatments will result in a decrease in the average period of admission?"
- "What is the relationship between profit gained by the shipments consisting of less than 10 items and the profit gained by the shipments of more than 10 items?"

It is clear that using traditional languages, such as SQL, to express these types of queries can be a very difficult task for inexperienced users. It is also clear that running these types of queries against operational databases would result in an unacceptably long response time.

The multidimensional model begins with the observation that the factors affecting decision-making processes are enterprise-specific facts, such as sales, shipments, hospital admissions, surgeries, and so on. Instances of a fact correspond to events that occurred. For example, every single sale or shipment carried out is an event. Each fact is described by the values of a set of relevant measures that provide a quantitative description of events. For example, sales receipts, amounts shipped, hospital admission costs, and surgery time are measures.

Obviously, a huge number of events occur in typical enterprises-too many to analyze one by one. Imagine placing them all into an n-dimensional space to help us quickly select and sort them out. The n-dimensional space axes are called analysis dimensions, and they define different perspectives to single out events. For example, the sales in a store chain can be represented in a three-dimensional space whose dimensions are products, stores, and dates. As far as shipments are concerned, products, shipment dates, orders, destinations, and terms & conditions can be used as dimensions. Hospital admissions can be defined by the department-date-patient combination, and would need to add the type of operation to classify surgery operations.

The concept of dimension gave life to the broadly used metaphor of cubes to represent multidimensional data. According to this metaphor, events are associated with cube cells and cube edges stand for analysis dimensions. If more than three dimensions exist, the cube is called a hypercube. Each cube cell is given a value for each measure. An intuitive representation of a cube in which the fact is a sale in a store chain. Its analysis dimensions are store, product and date. An event stands for a specific item sold in a specific store on a specific date, and it is described by two measures: the quantity sold and the receipts. This figure highlights that the cube is sparse-this means that many events did not actually take place. Of course, it cannot sell every item every day in every store.

Review Questions

1. What is KDD? Explain.
2. How the data warehousing helps for KDD in two important ways?
3. Briefly explain the basic steps of the KDD process.
4. Explain the Data Mining Tasks in detail.
5. What is supervised learning?
6. Give an example for Structural risk minimization
7. Explain various Data Mining Algorithms and Techniques.
8. Elaborate the data ware house architecture with diagram.
9. What is Data Staging and ETL?
10. Explain the Multidimensional model.

CHAPTER 2

CLUSTERING ANALYSIS

2.1. Clustering

Cluster analysis is an unsupervised learning method that constitutes a cornerstone of an intelligent data analysis process [Emamian V et al., 2012]. It is used for the exploration of inter relationships among a collection of patterns by organizing them into homogeneous clusters. It is called unsupervised learning because unlike classification no a priori labeling of patterns is available to use in categorizing others and inferring the cluster structure of the whole data.

Intra connectivity is a measure of the density of connections between the instances of a single cluster. High intra connectivity indicates a good clustering arrangement because the instances grouped within the same cluster are highly dependent on each other. Inter-connectivity is a measure of the connectivity between distinct clusters. A low degree of interconnectivity is desirable because it indicates that individual clusters are largely independent of each other.

Generally, clustering algorithms categorized into partitioning methods, hierarchical methods and density based methods, grid based methods and model based methods [He Zengyou et al., 2002; Deepti Sisodia et al., 2012].

Clustering is the task of exploratory data mining and used in many fields including pattern recognition, image analysis, information retrieval, machine learning and bioinformatics [He Z et al., 2003].

The appropriate clustering algorithm and parameter settings depend on the individual data set and intended use of the output. Cluster analysis is not an automatic task, but an iterative process of knowledge discovery that involves trial and failure.

2.2. Clustering Process

The clustering process may result in different partitioning of a data set, depending on the specific criterion used for clustering. Thus, there is a need of pre-processing before assuming a clustering task in a dataset.

The four basic steps to develop clustering process are represented in Fig 2.1 and summarized as follows.

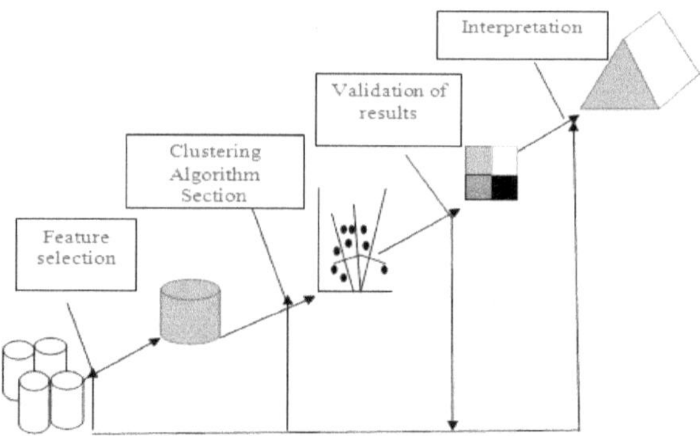

Fig. 2.1: Basic Steps of Clustering Process [He Z et al., 2003]

- **Feature selection:** The goal is to select properly the features on which clustering is to be performed so as to encode as much information as possible concerning the task of interest. Thus, pre-processing of data may be necessary prior to their utilization in clustering task.

- **Clustering algorithm:** This step refers to the choice of an algorithm output in the definition of a good clustering scheme for a dataset. A proximity measure and a clustering criterion mainly characterize a clustering algorithm as well as its efficiency to define a clustering scheme that fits the dataset [Hinneburg A and Keim D.A, 1998].

Proximity measure is a measure that quantifies similarity between two data points (i.e. feature vectors). In most of the cases, to ensure that all selected features contribute equally to the computation of the proximity measure and there are no features that dominate others.

Clustering criterion, this can be expressed via a cost function or some other type of rules. To take into account the type of clusters that are expected to occur in the data set. Thus, may define as "good" clustering criterion, leading to a partitioning that fit the data set well.

- **Validation of the results:** The correctness of clustering algorithm results is verified using appropriate criteria and techniques. Since clustering algorithms define clusters that are not known a priori, irrespective of the clustering methods the final partition of data requires some kind of evaluation in most applications.

- **Interpretation of the result:** In many cases, the experts in the application area have to integrate the clustering outputs with the experimental evidence and analysis in order to give the right conclusion.

In Table 2.1 shows the samples from the class room in which the number of students passed in the examination is listed out. These samples are grouped as failed students, mere pass and distinction students.

Table 2.1: Samples of Result (Pass % of Students)

Number of students	Marks
20	10
30	20
42	30
50	40
65	50
11	60
22	70
34	80

In Table 2.2 shows the clustered result in which the three clusters are shown with the corresponding samples.

Table 2.2: Samples after Clustering

Cluster	Number of students	Marks
	20	10
Cluster 1	30	20
	42	30
	50	40
Cluster 2	65	50
	11	60
Cluster 3	22	70
	34	80

There are many types of clustering techniques but there are two types of clustering such as Hierarchical Clustering and Partitional Clustering are discussed.

Clustering Methods

Clustering methods can be classified into the following categories

- Partitioning Method
- Hierarchical Method
- Density-based Method
- Grid-Based Method
- Model-Based Method
- Constraint-based Method

Partitioning Method

A database of 'n' objects and the partitioning method constructs 'k' partition of data. Each partition will represent a cluster and k ≤ n. It means that it will classify the data into k groups, which satisfy the following requirements

- Each group contains at least one object.
- Each object must belong to exactly one group.

Points to Remember

- For a given number of partitions (say k), the partitioning method will create an initial partitioning.
- Then it uses the iterative relocation technique to improve the partitioning by moving objects from one group to other.

Hierarchical Methods

This method creates a hierarchical decomposition of the given set of data objects. Classify hierarchical methods on the basis of how the hierarchical decomposition is formed. There are two approaches here

- Agglomerative Approach
- Divisive Approach

Agglomerative Approach

This approach is also known as the bottom-up approach. In this, start with each object forming a separate group. It keeps on merging the objects or groups that are close to one another. It keeps on doing so until all of the groups are merged into one or until the termination condition holds.

Divisive Approach

This approach is also known as the top-down approach. In this, start with all of the objects in the same cluster. In the continuous iteration, a cluster is split up into smaller clusters. It is down until each object in one cluster or the termination condition holds. This method is rigid, i.e., once a merging or splitting is done, it can never be undone.

Density-based Method

This method is based on the notion of density. The basic idea is to continue growing the given cluster as long as the density in the neighbourhood exceeds some threshold, i.e., for each data point within a given cluster, the radius of a given cluster has to contain at least a minimum number of points.

Grid-based Method

In this, the objects together form a grid. The object space is quantized into finite number of cells that form a grid structure.

Advantage

- The major advantage of this method is fast processing time.
- It is dependent only on the number of cells in each dimension in the quantized space.

Model-based Methods

In this method, a model is hypothesized for each cluster to find the best fit of data for a given model. This method locates the clusters by clustering the density function. It reflects spatial distribution of the data points.

This method also provides a way to automatically determine the number of clusters based on standard statistics, taking outlier or noise into account. It therefore yields robust clustering methods.

Constraint-based Method

In this method, the clustering is performed by the incorporation of user or application-oriented constraints. A constraint refers to the user expectation or the properties of desired clustering results. Constraints provide us with an interactive way of communication with the clustering process. Constraints can be specified by the user or the application requirement.

Clustering algorithms may be classified as listed below:

- Exclusive Clustering
- Overlapping Clustering
- Hierarchical Clustering
- Probabilistic Clustering

In the first case data are grouped in an exclusive way, so that if a certain datum belongs to a definite cluster then it could not be included in another cluster.

The second type, the overlapping clustering, uses fuzzy sets to cluster data, so that each point may belong to two or more clusters with different degrees of membership.

Hierarchical clustering algorithm is based on the union between the two nearest clusters. The beginning condition is realized by setting every datum as a cluster. After a few iterations it reaches the final clusters wanted. Finally, the last kind of clustering uses a completely probabilistic approach.

Each of these algorithms belongs to one of the clustering types listed above.

- K-means is an exclusive clustering algorithm
- Fuzzy C-means is an overlapping clustering algorithm
- Hierarchical clustering is obvious and lastly
- Mixture of Gaussian is a probabilistic clustering algorithm

2.3. Hierarchical Clustering

The Hierarchical clustering method group data instances into a tree of clusters [Chatzigiannakis V et al., 2006]. There are two major methods under this category. One is the agglomerative method, which forms the clusters in a bottom up fashion until all data instances belong to the same cluster. The other is the divisive method which splits up the data set into smaller cluster in a top down fashion until each cluster contains only one instance. Both divisive algorithm and agglomerative algorithm can be represented by dendrograms. The idea of this method is to build a hierarchy of clusters showing relations between the individual members and merging clusters of data based on similarity. In the first step of clustering, the algorithm looks for the two most similar data points and merge them to create a new "pseudo-data point", which represents the average of the two merged data points. Each iterative step takes the next two closest data points (or pseudo-data points) and merges them. This process is generally continued until there is one large cluster containing all the original data points. Hierarchical clustering results in a "tree", shows the relationship of all of the original points.

Clustering is an unsupervised learning method: there is no target value (class label) to be predicted, the goal is finding common patterns or grouping similar examples.

- Differences between models/algorithms for clustering:
- Conceptual (model-based) vs. partitioning
- Exclusive vs. overlapping
- Deterministic vs. probabilistic
- Hierarchical vs. flat
- Incremental vs. batch learning

Evaluating clustering quality: subjective approaches, objective functions (e.g. category utility, entropy).

Major Approaches

- **Cluster/2:** flat, conceptual (model-based), batch learning, possibly overlapping, deterministic.

- **Partitioning methods:** flat, batch learning, exclusive, deterministic or probabilistic. Algorithms: k-means, probability-based clustering (EM)

Hierarchical Clustering

- Partitioning: agglomerative (bottom-up) or divisible (top-down).
- Conceptual: Cobweb, category utility function.

One of the first conceptual clustering approaches [Michalski, 1983].

- Works as a meta-learning scheme - uses a learning algorithm in its inner loop to form categories.
- Has no practical value, but introduces important ideas and techniques, used in current approaches to conceptual clustering. The CLUSTER/2 algorithm forms k categories by constructing individual objects grouped around k seed objects. It works as follows:
  - Select k objects (seeds) from the set of observed objects (randomly or using some selection function).
  - For each seed, using it as a positive example the all the other seeds as negative examples, find a maximally general description that covers all positive and none of the negative examples.
  - Classify all objects form the sample in categories according to these descriptions. Then replace each maximally general description with a maximally specific one that covers all objects in the category. (This possibly avoids category overlapping.)
  - If there are still overlapping categories, then using some metric (e.g. Euclidean distance) find central objects in each category and repeat steps 1-3 using these objects as seeds.
  - Stop when some quality criterion for the category descriptions is satisfied. Such a criterion might be the complexity of the descriptions (e.g. the number of conjuncts)
  - If there is no improvement of the categories after several steps, then choose new seeds using another criterion (e.g. the objects near the edge of the category).

However, both methods suffer from their inability to perform adjustments once the splitting or merging decision is made. Advantages are:

- Does not require the number of clusters to be known in advance.
- Computes a complete hierarchy of clusters.
- Good result visualizations are integrated into the methods.
- A "flat" partition can be derived afterwards.

Hierarchical clustering techniques use various criteria to decide "locally" at each step which clusters should be joined (or split for divisive approaches). For agglomerative hierarchical techniques, the criterion is typically to merge the "closest" pair of clusters where "close" is defined by a specified measure of cluster proximity.

There are three definitions of the closeness between two clusters: single link, complete link and average link.

- **Single link** similarity between two clusters is the similarity between the two most similar instances one of which appears in each cluster. Single link is good at handling non-elliptical shapes but is sensitive to noise and outliers.
- **Complete link** similarity is the similarity between the two most dissimilar instances one from each cluster.
- **Average link** is less susceptible to noise and outliers but can break large clusters and has trouble with convex shapes. The average link similarity is a compromise between the two.

2.3.1. Advantages of Hierarchical Clustering

- Embedded flexibility regarding the level of granularity
- Ease of handling of any forms of similarity or distance
- Consequently, applicability to any attributes types
- Hierarchical clustering outputs a hierarchy, i.e. a structure that is more informative than the unstructured set of flat clusters returned by k-means. Therefore, it is easier to decide on the number of clusters by looking at the dendrogram.
- Easy to implement

2.3.2. Disadvantages of Hierarchical Clustering

- Vagueness of termination criteria
- It is not possible to undo the previous step: once the instances have been assigned to a cluster, they can no longer be moved around.
- Time complexity: not suitable for large datasets
- Initial seeds have a strong impact on the final results
- The order of the data has an impact on the final results
- Very sensitive to outliers

The fact that most hierarchical algorithms do not revisit once constructed (intermediate) clusters with the purpose of their improvement.

2.4.   Partitional Clustering

Partitional clustering decomposes data set into a set of disjoint clusters. Given a data set of n points, a partitioning method constructs k (n ≥ k) partitions of the data, with each partition representing a cluster.

Partitioning methods are divided into two major subcategories, the centroid and the medoids algorithms. The centroid algorithms represent each cluster by using the gravity centre of the instances. The medoid algorithms represent each cluster by means of the instances closest to the gravity centre. The most well-known centroid algorithm is the k-means [Jain A.K et al., 1999]. The k-means method partitions the data set into k subsets such that all points in a given subset are closest to the same centre. It randomly selects k of the instances to represent the clusters. Based on the selected attributes, all remaining instances are assigned to their closer centre. Iterative distance-based clustering.

- Used by statisticians for decades.
- Similarly to Cluster/2 uses k seeds (predefined k), but is based on a distance measure:
    - Select k instances (cluster centers) from the sample (usually at random).
    - Assign instances to clusters according to their distance to the cluster centers.
    - Find new cluster centers and go to step 2 until the process converges (i.e. the same instances are assigned to each cluster in two consecutive passes).
- The clustering depends greatly on the initial choice of cluster centers the algorithm may fall in a local minimum.
- Example of bad choice of cluster centers: four instances at the vertices of a rectangle, two initial cluster centers – midpoints of the long sides of the rectangle. This is a stable configuration, however not a good clustering.
- Solution to the local minimum problem: restart the algorithm with another set of cluster centers.
- Hierarchical k-means: apply k = 2 recursively to the resulting clusters.

K-means then computes the new centers by taking the mean of all data points belonging to the same cluster. The operation is iterated until there is no change in the gravity centre. If k cannot be known ahead of time, various values of k can be evaluated until the most suitable one is found. The effectiveness of this method as well as of others relies heavily on the objective function used in measuring the distance between instances. The difficulty is in finding a distance measure that works well with all types of data. There are several approaches to define the distance between instances [Jain A.K et al., 1999].

The k-means algorithm has the following important properties:

- It is efficient in processing large data sets.
- It often terminates at a local optimum.
- The clusters have spherical shapes.
- It is sensitive to noise.

The algorithm described above is classified as a batch method because it requires that all the data should be available in advance. However, there are variants of the k-means clustering process, which gets around this limitation [Jain A.K et al., 1999]. Choosing the proper initial centroids is the key step of the basic k means procedure. The k-modes algorithm [Huang Z, 1998] is a recent partitioning algorithm and uses the simple matching coefficient measure to deal with categorical attributes.

The k-prototypes algorithm [Huang Z, 1998], through the definition of a combined dissimilarity measure, further integrates the k-means and k-modes algorithms to allow for clustering instances described by mixed attributes. Another generalization of conventional k-means clustering algorithm has been presented [Yiu-Ming Cheung, 2003]. This new one applicable to ellipse-shaped data clusters as well as ball-shaped ones without dead-unit problem, but also performs correct clustering without pre-determining the exact cluster number. It classifies the data into k groups by satisfying the following requirements:

- Each group contains at least one point.
- Each point belongs to exactly one group.

Partitioning methods relocate instances by moving them from one cluster to another, starting from an initial partitioning. Such methods typically require that the number of clusters will be pre-set by the user. To achieve global optimality in partitioned based clustering, an exhaustive enumeration process of all possible partitions is required. Many partition clustering algorithms to minimize an objective function. For example, in k-means and k-medoids the function (also referred to as the distortion function) is given by the equation.

$$\sum_{i=1}^{k} \sum_{j=1}^{|C_i|} \left(\text{Dist} \left(x_j, \text{center}(i) \right) \right)$$

where $| C_i |$ is the number of points in cluster i, $\text{Dist}(x_j, \text{center}(i))$ is the distance between point x_j and center i. Many distance function can be used, such as Euclidean distance and L_1 norm. Partitioning algorithms are based on specifying an initial number of groups and iteratively reallocating objects among groups to convergence. This algorithm typically determines all clusters at once. In Table 2.3 describes the comparison of hierarchical clustering and partitional clustering.

Table 2.3: Differences between Hierarchical and Partitional Clustering

[Deepti Sisodia et al., 2012]

S. No.	Parameter	Hierarchical	Partition
1	Running Time	Slower	Faster
2	Assumptions	Needs only a similarity measures	Needs stronger Assumptions
3	Input Parameter	Not require	Need number of cluster
4	Output	Meaningful and subjective division of clusters	K clusters
5	Efficiency	Comparatively less	Comparatively more
6	Suited	Suited for categorical and non linear data	Not Suited for categorical and non linear data

Density based methods which is the main concern of the thesis belong to partitional clustering [Smith R et al., 2002]. The density based clusters are defined as clusters which are differentiated from other clusters by varying densities that means a group which have dense region of objects may be surrounded by low density regions [Ram S et al., 2010].

2.5. Probability-Based Clustering

Why probabilities?

- Restricted amount of evidence implies probabilistic reasoning.
- From a probabilistic perspective, want to find the most likely clusters given the data.
- An instance only has certain probability of belonging to a particular cluster.

Probability-based Clustering–Mixture Models

- For a single attribute: three parameters - mean, standard deviation and sampling probability.
- Each cluster A is defined by a mean (μA) and a standard deviation (A).
- Samples are taken from each cluster A with a specified probability of sampling P (A).
- Finite mixture problem: given a dataset, find the mean, standard deviation and the probability of sampling for each cluster.

Research Background

In traditional markets, customer clustering/segmentation is one of the most significant methods used in studies of marketing. This study classifies existing customer cluster/ segmentation methods into methodology-oriented and application-oriented approaches.

Most methodology driven studies used mathematical methodologies; e.g statistics, neural net, generic algorithm (GA) and Fuzzy set to identify the optimized segmented homogenous group. In recent years, it has been recognized that the partitioned clustering technique is well suited for clustering a large dataset due to their relatively low computational requirements. Behavioral clustering and segmentation help derive strategic marketing initiatives by using the variables that determine customer shareholder value. By conducting demographic clustering and segmentation within the behavioral segments, it can define tactical marketing campaigns and select the appropriate marketing channel and advertising for the tactical campaign. It is then possible to target those customers most likely to exhibit the desired behavior by creating predictive models.

In this work demographic clustering algorithm is used to identify the customer clustering. In phase 1, the customer data is cleansed and developed patterns using various parameters and subsequently, in phase 2 profiled the data, developed the clusters and identified the high-value low risk customers. From the experimental results it showed that the proposed approach would generate more useful pattern from large data.

2.6. Data Mining and Clustering Methods

Data mining-also known as knowledge-discovery in databases(KDD) is process of extracting potentially useful information from raw data. A software engine can scan large amounts of data and automatically report interesting patterns without requiring human intervention. Other knowledge discovery technologies are Statistical Analysis, OLAP, Data Visualization, and Ad hoc queries. Unlike these technologies, data mining does not require a human to ask specific questions. In general, Data mining has four major relationships.

They are:

i. Classes

ii. Clusters

iii. Associations

iv. Sequential patterns.

(i) Classes: Stored data is used to locate data in predetermined groups. For example, a restaurant chain could mine customer purchase data to determine when customers visit and what they typically order. This information could be used to increase traffic by having daily specials.

(ii) Clusters: Data items are grouped according to logical relationships or consumer preferences. For example, data can be mined to identify market segments or consumer affinities.

(iii) Associations: Data can be mined to identify associations. The beer-diaper example is an example of associative mining.

(iv) Sequential patterns: Data is mined to anticipate behavior patterns and trends. For example, an outdoor equipment retailer could predict the likelihood of a backpack being purchased based on a consumer's purchase of sleeping bags and hiking shoes.

2.6.1. Clustering Methods

Clustering is a typical unsupervised learning technique for grouping similar data points. A clustering algorithm assigns a large number of data points to a smaller number of groups such that data points in the same group share the same properties while, in different groups, they are dissimilar.

Clustering has many applications, including part family formation for group technology, image segmentation, information retrieval, web pages grouping, market segmentation, and scientific and engineering analysis.

Many clustering methods have been proposed and they can be broadly classified into four categories: partitioning methods, hierarchical methods, density-based methods and grid based methods. Other clustering techniques that do not fit in these categories have been developed. They are fuzzy clustering, artificial neural networks and generic algorithms. The following section deals the customer clustering.

2.6.2. Customer Clustering

Customer clustering is the most important data mining methodologies used in marketing and customer relationship management (CRM). Customer clustering would use customer-purchase transaction data to track buying behavior and create strategic business initiatives. Companies want to keep high-profit, high-value, and low-risk customers. This cluster typically represents the 10 to 20 percent of customers who create 50 to 80 percent of a company's profits. A company would not want to lose these customers, and the strategic initiative for the segment is obviously retention. A low-profit, high-value, and low-risk customer segment is also an attractive one, and the obvious goal here would be to increase profitability for this segment. Cross-selling (selling new products) and up-selling (selling more of what customers currently buy) to this segment are the marketing initiatives of choice.

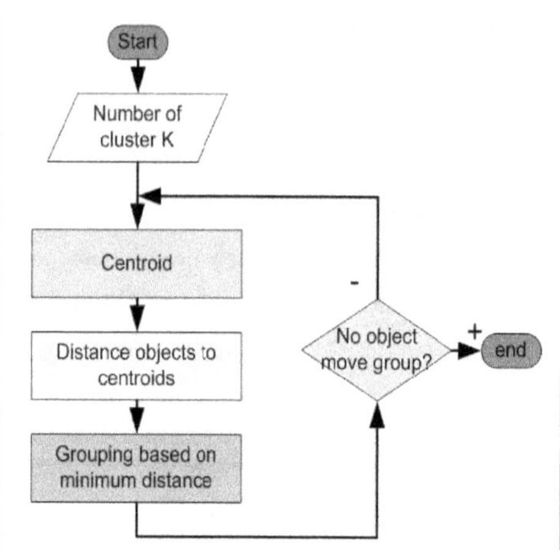

Fig. 2.2: K-Means Clustering

Simply speaking it is an algorithm to classify or to group your objects based on attributes/ features into K number of group. K is positive integer number. The grouping is done by minimizing the sum of squares of distances between data and the corresponding cluster centroid. Thus, the purpose of K-mean clustering is to classify the data.

Numerical Example (Manual Calculation)

The basic step of k-means clustering is simple. In the beginning, it determines number of cluster K and assumes the centroid or center of these clusters. This can take any random objects as the initial centroids or the first K objects can also serve as the initial centroids. Then the K means algorithm will do the three steps below until convergence Iterate until stable (= no object move group):

1. Determine the centroid coordinate.
2. Determine the distance of each object to the centroids.
3. Group the object based on minimum distance (find the closest centroid).

Data clustering techniques are descriptive data analysis techniques that can be applied to multivariate data sets to uncover the structure present in the data. They are particularly useful when classical second order statistics (the sample mean and covariance) cannot be used. Namely, in exploratory data analysis, one of the assumptions that is made is that no prior knowledge about the dataset, and therefore the dataset's distribution, is available. In such a situation, data clustering can be a valuable tool. Data clustering is a form of unsupervised classification, as the clusters are formed by evaluating similarities and dissimilarities of intrinsic characteristics between different cases, and the grouping of cases is based on those emergent similarities and not on an external criterion. Also, these techniques can be useful for datasets of any dimensionality over three, as it is very difficult for humans to compare items of such complexity reliably without a support to aid the comparison.

The technique presented in this tutorial, k-means clustering, belongs to partitioning-based techniques grouping, which are based on the iterative relocation of data points between clusters. It is used to divide either the cases or the variables of a dataset into non-overlapping groups, or clusters, based on the characteristics uncovered. Whether the algorithm is applied to the cases or the variables of the dataset depends on which dimensions of this dataset that want to reduce the dimensionality of. The goal is to produce groups of cases/variables with a high degree of similarity within each group and a low degree of similarity between groups (Hastie, Tibshirani & Friedman, 2001). The k-means clustering technique can also be described as a centroid model as one vector representing the mean is used to describe each cluster. [MacQueen, (1967)] the creator of one of the k-means algorithms presented in this phase, considered the main use of k-means clustering to be more of a way for researchers to gain qualitative and quantitative insight into large multivariate data sets than a way to find a unique and definitive grouping for the data.

K-means clustering is very useful in exploratory data analysis and data mining in any field of research, and as the growth in computer power has been followed by a growth in the occurrence of large data sets. Its ease of implementation, computational efficiency and low memory consumption has kept the k-means clustering very popular, even compared to other clustering techniques. Such other clustering techniques include connectivity models like hierarchical clustering methods (Hastie, Tibshirani & Friedman, 2000). These have the advantage of allowing for an unknown number of clusters to be searched for in the data, but are very costly computationally due to the fact that they are based on the dissimilarity matrix. Also included in cluster analysis methods are distribution models like expectation-maximisation algorithms and density models (Ankerst, Breunig, Kriegel & Sander, 1999).

A secondary goal of k-means clustering is the reduction of the complexity of the data. A good example would be letter grades (Faber, 1994). The numerical grades are clustered into the letters and represented by the average included in each class.

Finally, k-means clustering can also be used as an initialization step for more computationally expensive algorithms like Learning Vector Quantization or Gaussian Mixtures, thus giving an approximate separation of the data as a starting point and reducing the noise present in the dataset (Shannon, 1948).

A good cluster analysis is both efficient and effective, in that it uses as few clusters as possible while still capturing all statistically important clusters. Similarity in cluster analysis is usually taken as meaning "proximity", and elements closer to one another in the input space are considered more similar.

Analysis of K-means Clustering

Present three k-means clustering algorithms: The Forgy/Lloyd algorithm, the MacQueen algorithm and the Hartigan & Wong algorithm. Chose those three algorithms because they are the most widely used k-means clustering techniques and they all have slightly different goals and thus results. To be able to use any of the three, you first need to know how many clusters are present in your data. As this information is often unavailable, multiple trials will be necessary to find the best amount of clusters. As a starting point, it is often useful to standardize the data if the components of the cases are not in the same scale. There is no absolute best algorithm. The choice of the optimal algorithm depends on the characteristics of the dataset (size, number of variables in the cases). Jain, Duin & Mao (2000) even suggest trying several different clustering algorithms to gain the best understanding possible about the dataset.

Forgy/Lloyd algorithm

The Lloyd algorithm (1957, published 1982) and the Forgy's algorithm (1965) are both batch (also called offline) centroid models. A centroid is the geometric center of a convex object and can be thought of as a generalization of the mean. Batch algorithms are algorithms where a transformative step is applied to all cases at once. They are well suited to analyze large data sets, since the incremental k-means algorithms require to store the cluster membership of each case or to do two nearest-cluster computations as each case is processed, which is computationally expensive on large datasets. The difference between the Lloyd algorithm and the Forgy algorithm is that the Lloyd algorithm considers the data distribution discrete while the Forgy algorithm considers the distribution continuous. They have exactly the same procedure apart from that consideration.

MacQueen Algorithm

The MacQueen algorithm (1967) is an iterative (also called online or incremental) algorithm. The main difference with Forgy/Lloyd's algorithm is that the centroids are recalculated every time a case change subspace and also after each pass through all cases. The centroids are initialized the same way as in the Forgy/Lloyd algorithm and the iterations are as follow. For each case in turn, if the centroid of the subspace it currently belongs to is the nearest, no change is made. If another centroid is the closest, the case is reassigned to the other centroid and the centroids for both the old and new subspaces are recalculated as the mean of the belonging cases. The algorithm is more efficient as it updates centroids more often and usually needs to perform one complete pass through the cases to converge on a solution.

Here is the pseudo code describing the iterations:

1. Choose the number of clusters
2. Choose the metric to use
3. Choose the method to pick initial centroids
4. Assign initial centroids
5. While metric(centroids, cases)>threshold
    a. For i <= cases
        i. Assign case i to closest cluster according to metric
        ii. Recalculate centroids for the two affected clusters
    b. Recalculate centroids

Hartigan & Wong Algorithm

This algorithm searches for the partition of data space with locally optimal within-cluster sum of squares of errors (SSE). It means that it may assign a case to another subspace, even if it currently belong to the subspace of the closest centroid, if doing so minimizes the total within-cluster sum of square (see below). The cluster centers are initialized the same way as in the Forgy/Lloyd algorithm. The cases are then assigned to the centroid nearest them and the centroids are calculated as the mean of the assigned data points. The iterations are as follows. If the centroid has been updated in the last step, for each data point included, the within-cluster sum of squares for each data point if included in another cluster is calculated. If one of the cluster sum of square (SSE2 in the equation below, for all $i \neq 1$) is smaller than the current one (SSE1), the case is assigned to this new cluster.

Here is the pseudo code describing the iterations:

1. Choose the number of clusters
2. Choose the metric to use
3. Choose the method to pick initial centroids
4. Assign initial centroids
5. Assign cases to closest centroid
6. Calculate centroids
7. For j <= nb clusters, if centroid j was updated last iteration

a. Calculate SSE within cluster

b. For i <= nb cases in cluster

i. Compute SSE for cluster $k \mathrel{!}= j$ if case included

ii. If SSE cluster k < SSE cluster j, case change cluster

Alternate Algorithms

Optimisation of the algorithms usage: While the algorithms presented are very efficient, since the technique is often used as a first classifier on large datasets, any optimisation that speeds the convergence of the clustering is useful. Bottou and Bengio (1995) have found that the fastest convergence on a solution is usually obtained by using an online algorithm for the first iteration through the entire dataset and an off-line algorithm subsequently as needed. This comes from the fact that online k-means benefits from the redundancies of the k training set and improve the centroids by going through a few cases (depending on the amount of redundancies) as much as would a full iteration through the offline algorithm (Bengio,1991).

For very large datasets: For very large datasets that would make the computation of the previous algorithms too computationally expensive, it is possible to choose a random sample from the whole population of cases and apply the algorithm on the sample. If the sample is sufficiently large, the distribution of these initial reference points should reflect the distribution of cases in the entire set.

Fuzzy k-means clustering: In fuzzy k-means clustering (Bezdek, 1981), each case has a set of degree of belonging relative to all clusters. It differs from previously presented k-means clustering where each case belongs only to one cluster at a time. In this algorithm, the centroid of a cluster (ck) is the mean of all cases in the dataset, weighted by their degree of belonging to the cluster (wk).

Self-Organising Maps: Self-Organizing Maps (Kohonen, 1982) are an artificial neural network algorithm that aims to extract attributes present in a dataset and transcribe them into an output space of lower dimensionality, while keeping the spatial structure of the data. Doing so clusters similar cases on the map, a process that can be likened to the k-means algorithm clustering centroids. This neural network has two layers, the input layer which is the initial dataset, and an output layer that is the self-organizing map, which is usually bidimensional. There is a connection weight between each variable (or attribute) of a case and the map, thus making the connection weights matrix of the dimensionality of the input multiplied by the dimensionality of the map. It uses a Hebbian competitive learning algorithm. What is obtained at the end is a map where similar elements are contiguous, which also give a two dimensional representation of the data. It is therefore useful if a graphic representation of the data is advantageous to its comprehension.

Model-based Clustering Methods

These methods attempt to optimize the fit between the given data and some mathematical models. Unlike conventional clustering, which identifies groups of objects; model-based clustering methods also find characteristic descriptions for each group, where each group represents a concept or class. The most frequently used induction methods are decision trees and neural networks.

Decision Trees. In decision trees, the data is represented by a hierarchical tree, where each leaf refers to a concept and contains a probabilistic description of that concept. Several algorithms produce classification trees for representing the unlabelled data. The most well-known algorithms are: COBWEB—this algorithm assumes that all attributes are independent (an often too naive assumption). Its aim is to achieve high predictability of nominal variable values, given a cluster. This algorithm is not suitable for clustering large database data (Fisher, 1987). CLASSIT, an extension of COBWEB for continuous-valued data, unfortunately has similar problems as the COBWEB algorithm.

Neural Networks. This type of algorithm represents each cluster by a neuron or "prototype". The input data is also represented by neurons, which are connected to the prototype neurons. Each such connection has a weight, which is learned adaptively during learning. A very popular neural algorithm for clustering is the self-organizing map (SOM). This algorithm constructs a single-layered network. The learning process takes place in a "winner-takes-all" fashion: The prototype neurons compete for the current instance. The winner is the neuron whose weight vector is closest to the instance currently presented. The winner and its neighbors learn by having their weights adjusted.

The SOM algorithm is successfully used for vector quantization and speech recognition. It is useful for visualizing high-dimensional data in 2D or 3D space. However, it is sensitive to the initial selection of weight vector, as well as to its different parameters, such as the learning rate and neighborhood radius.

Grid-based Methods: These methods partition the space into a finite number of cells that form a grid structure on which all of the operations for clustering are performed. The main advantage of the approach is its fast processing time (Han and Kamber, 2001).

Soft-computing Methods: Section 5.4.2 described the usage of neural networks in clustering tasks. This section further discusses the important usefulness of other soft-computing methods in clustering tasks.

Fuzzy Clustering. Traditional clustering approaches generate partitions; in a partition, each instance belongs to one and only one cluster. Hence, the clusters in a hard clustering are disjointed. Fuzzy clustering (see for instance (Hoppner, 2005)) extends this notion and suggests a soft clustering schema. In this case, each pattern is associated with every cluster using some sort of membership function, namely, each cluster is a fuzzy set of all the patterns. Larger membership values indicate higher confidence in the assignment of the pattern to the cluster. A hard clustering can be obtained from a fuzzy partition by using a threshold of the membership value. The most popular fuzzy clustering algorithm is the fuzzy c-means (FCM) algorithm. Even though it is better than the hard K-means algorithm at avoiding local minima, FCM can still converge to local minima of the squared error criterion. The design of membership functions is the most important problem in fuzzy clustering; different choices include those based on similarity decomposition and centroids of clusters. A generalization of the FCM algorithm has been proposed through a family of objective functions. A fuzzy c-shell algorithm and an adaptive variant for detecting circular and elliptical boundaries have been presented.

Evolutionary Approaches for Clustering. Evolutionary techniques are stochastic general purpose methods for solving optimization problems. Since clustering problem can be defined as an optimization problem, evolutionary approaches may be appropriate here. The idea is to use evolutionary operators and a population of clustering structures to converge into a globally optimal clustering. Candidate clustering are encoded as chromosomes. The most commonly used evolutionary operators are: selection, recombination, and mutation. A fitness function evaluated on a chromosome determines a chromosome's likelihood of surviving into the next generation. The most frequently used evolutionary technique in clustering problems is genetic algorithms (GAs). A fitness value is associated with each clusters structure. A higher fitness value indicates a better cluster structure. A suitable fitness function is the inverse of the squared error value. Cluster structures with a small squared error will have a larger fitness value.

Input: S (instance set), K (number of clusters), n (population size)

Output: clusters

1: Randomly create a population of n structures; each corresponds to valid K-clusters of the data.

2: repeat

3: Associate a fitness value 8structure 2 population.

4: Regenerate a new generation of structures.

5: until some termination condition is satisfied.

The most obvious way to represent structures is to use strings of length m (where m is the number of instances in the given set). The i-th entry of the string denotes the cluster to which the i-th instance belongs. Consequently, each entry can have values from 1 to K. An improved representation scheme is proposed where an additional separator symbol is used along with the pattern labels to represent a partition. Using this representation permits them to map the clustering problem into a permutation problem such as the travelling salesman problem, which can be solved by using the permutation crossover operators. This solution also suffers from permutation redundancy.

In GAs, a selection operator propagates solutions from the current generation to the next generation based on their fitness. Selection employs a probabilistic scheme so that solutions with higher fitness have a higher probability of getting reproduced. There are a variety of recombination operators in use; crossover is the most popular. Crossover takes as input a pair of chromosomes (called parents) and outputs a new pair of chromosomes (called children or offspring). In this way the GS explores the search space. Mutation is used to make sure that the algorithm is not trapped in local optimum. More recently investigated is the use of edge-based crossover to solve the clustering problem. Here, all patterns in a cluster are assumed to form a complete graph by connecting them with edges. Offspring are generated from the parents so that they inherit the edges from their parents. In a hybrid approach that has been proposed, the GAs is used only to find good initial cluster centers and the K-means algorithm is applied to find the final partition. This hybrid approach performed better than the GAs.

A major problem with GAs is their sensitivity to the selection of various parameters such as population size, crossover and mutation probabilities, etc. Several researchers have studied this problem and suggested guidelines for selecting these control parameters. However, these guidelines may not yield good results on specific problems like pattern clustering. It was reported that hybrid genetic algorithms incorporating problem-specific heuristics are good for clustering. A similar claim is made about the applicability of GAs to other practical problems. Another issue with GAs is the selection of an appropriate representation which is low in order and short in defining length. There are other evolutionary techniques such as evolution strategies (ESs), and evolutionary programming (EP). These techniques differ from the GAs in solution representation and the type of mutation operator used; EP does not use a recombination operator, but only selection and mutation. Each of these three approaches has been used to solve the clustering problem by viewing it as a minimization of the squared error criterion. Some of the theoretical issues, such as the convergence of these approaches, were studied. GAs perform a globalized search for solutions whereas most other clustering procedures per form a localized search. In a localized search, the solution obtained at the 'next iteration' of the procedure is in the vicinity of the current solution. In this sense, the K-means algorithm and fuzzy clustering algorithms are all localized search techniques. In the case of GAs, the crossover and mutation operators can produce new solutions that are completely different from the current ones.

It is possible to search for the optimal location of the centroids rather than finding the optimal partition. This idea permits the use of ESs and EP, because centroids can be coded easily in both these approaches, as they support the direct representation of a solution as a real-valued vector. ESs was used on both hard and fuzzy clustering problems and EP has been used to evolve fuzzy min-max clusters. It has been observed that they perform better than their classical counterparts, the K-means algorithm and the fuzzy c-means algorithm. However, all of these approaches are over sensitive to their parameters. Consequently, for each specific problem, the user is required to tune the parameter values to suit the application.

Simulated Annealing for Clustering. Another general-purpose stochastic search technique that can be used for clustering is simulated annealing (SA), which is a sequential stochastic search technique designed to avoid local optima. This is accomplished by accepting with some probability a new solution for the next iteration of lower quality (as measured by the criterion function). The probability of acceptance is governed by a critical parameter called the temperature (by analogy with annealing in metals), which is typically specified in terms of a starting (first iteration) and final temperature value. Selim and Al-Sultan (1991) studied the effects of control parameters on the performance of the algorithm. SA is statistically guaranteed to find the global optimal solution.

The SA algorithm can be slow in reaching the optimal solution, because optimal results require the temperature to be decreased very slowly from iteration to iteration. Tabu search, like SA, is a method designed to cross boundaries of feasibility or local optimality and to systematically impose and release constraints to permit exploration of otherwise forbidden regions. Al-Sultan (1995) suggests using Tabu search as an alternative to SA.

2.7.   Clustering Algorithms for Ad Hoc Wireless Networks

An ad hoc network is a multichip wireless communication network supporting mobile users without any existing infrastructure. To become commercially successful, the technology must allow networks to support many users. A complication is that addressing and routing in ad hoc networks does not scale up as easily as in the Internet. By introducing hierarchical addresses to ad hoc networks, it can electively address this complication. Clustering provides a method to build and maintain hierarchical addresses in ad hoc networks. Here, survey several clustering algorithms, concentrating on those that are based on graph domination. In addition, describe results that show that building clustered hierarchies is adorable and that clustering algorithms can also be used to build virtual backbones to enhance network quality of service. Kleinrock described ad hoc net-working technology as a blend of nomadicity, embeddedness, and ubiquity. In a network of the future, users and computing devices will be able to connect to such a network conveniently and even transparently. Computing and communication capabilities will not only be restricted to standard electronic devices, but every gadget can a_ord to embed a considerable amount of intelligence. On a global basis, devices in the network will be able to rely on other devices to relay packets for them if necessary. The entire world will be heterogeneously networked by a vast\invisible global infrastructure". The idea of ad hoc networking has been around for over 30 years. As early as 1972, DARPA started the pioneering PRNet (Packet Radio Network) project. Subsequently, various projects sponsored by the military, such as SURAN (Survivable Radio Networks), TI (Tactical Internet), and GloMo (Global Mobile Information Systems), were launched to implement the ad hoc networking paradigm. In the meantime, many enabling technologies, such as wireless signal processing and encoding, distributed computing, VLSI circuit design and manufacturing, cryptography, positioning services, et al. have been invented and developed that can address various problems confronting the ad hoc network community. Given the successful commercial use of the Internet, one cannot help asking why there are no cost-effective the-shelf commercial ad hoc networking systems. Among the many challenges for ad hoc network designers and users, scalability is a critical issue. In particular, when a topology network contains a large number of nodes, control overhead, such as routing packets, requires a large percentage of the limited wireless bandwidth.

A technology can be sustainably viable only if it can widespread use. In order to allow ad hoc networks to achieve commercial success, it must solve the scalability problem. One promising approach is to build hierarchies among the nodes, such that the network topology can be abstracted. This process is commonly referred to as clustering and the substructures that are collapsed in higher levels are called clusters.

Here, explains why scalability is a hindrance for ad hoc networks and why the scaling techniques used successfully by the Internet are not directly applicable. Then survey some of the clustering algorithms for building network hierarchies. Finally, consider the costs associated with using clusters in hierarchical routing and how QoS in ad hoc networks can benefit from clustering. Scalability Perkins observed that aggregating routing information is the key to Internet scalability". In particular, a node's IP address contains hierarchical information related to its location that can be used in routing. Due to the mobility of nodes in an ad hoc network, this is not as simple to accomplish. In a multichip packet-switched network, intermediate nodes are required to route packets between the source and destination if they (the source and the destination) are not directly connected. For example, in a distance-vector routing protocol, each node participating in the route calculation stores a routing table and shares it with all neighboring nodes. If the network has a topology (that is, all nodes are treated equally), the size of the routing table is proportional to the number of nodes in the entire network. Further, as network size increases, communication costs tend to consume a larger proportion of the bandwidth. Furthermore, as the rate of the network topology change increases, the exchange of routing tables between neighboring nodes must be more frequent to keep the routing information up to date. Other network parameters, such as network node density and traffic load, can also impair network scalability. Arpacioglu, Small, and Haas have begun a study of the scalability issue of multihop networks and, in particular, ad hoc networks.

The Internet, a multihop packet-switched communication network, manages to function with approximately 109 nodes. Each node in the Internet is given a 32-bit IP address that is assigned in a way such that all the nodes in the same subnet share the same address pre. Unfortunately, due to mobility, nodes in an ad hoc network cannot be assigned such aggregate addresses. This is an obstacle for scaling up ad hoc networks. However, believe that many substructures in a large-scale, even global, ad hoc network are relatively stable. Users can indeed be mobile, but their movements are usually connected within a special geographical area. For example, students may wander around a campus during the day and commute within a metropolitan area on a daily basis. These movements cause local topology changes but do not drastically alter the overall structure of the network. Since many of these changes are connected to a relatively small region, one can abstract the network to obtain a simpler topology and avoid the need to inform the entire network of these topology changes. Local portions of the network are represented by super-vertices in the abstracted topology and connections between them are super-edges. Clustering is a process of defining such an abstracted structure of a network. It can be applied recursively to obtain a multi-level hierarchy.

2.8.   A Secure Clustering Algorithm in Mobile Ad Hoc Networks

A mobile ad hoc network (MANET) is the cooperative engagement of a collection of wireless mobile nodes without any predefined infrastructure relied on to keep the network connected. As ad hoc networks do not have any fixed infrastructure, all network functions can be performed by the mobile nodes themselves in a self-organizing manner. This gives rise to much vulnerability in ad hoc networks, making the issue of security very important and challenging. With the growth of ad hoc networks, the hierarchical structure has been receiving a much attention due to its scalability in large-scale networks. In recent years, many kinds of clustering algorithms are proposed to elect the backbone nodes and build cluster. According to the various objectives and requirements, clustering schemes focus on different metrics, such as the node's mobility, energy, connection and load balance. The lowest-ID cluster algorithm the highest-degree cluster algorithm and the weighted clustering algorithm are the typical clustering algorithms. Currently, most clustering algorithms assume that the network environment is reliable and has no threats. In fact, ad hoc networks are easy to be wiretapped, intruded and attacked, because of the open distributed network structure. Cluster head and gateway are the key nodes (i.e., backbone nodes) in hierarchical ad hoc networks. If they are intruded, the network performance must decrease seriously. Therefore, need to promote an effective detection measure to the bone cluster structure for network security, such as clustering in hierarchical ad hoc networks. Author proposes a secure clustering algorithm based on reputation (SCAR). The nodes' reputation is used to improve security, which is evaluated by combining the experience of the node in the routing process. In addition, consider degree and relative mobility in the clustering to guarantee the stability of clusters. The weight of each node is computed through considering the above three factors simultaneously. It is used to elect the secure backbone nodes in the networks. Moreover, it is efficient in the cluster rebuilding and healing.

Clustering Algorithm

A secure clustering algorithm SCAR, which takes into account a combined weight metric, including the reputation value, the node' degree [9] and the relative mobility. The weight is calculated as follow.

Cluster Head Election

In the initial of establishing cluster, the nodes are assigned as the role (i.e., cluster head, gateway and cluster member) in the cluster through the clustering procedure. Each node broadcasts Hello message to its neighbor nodes periodically for connectivity. In this algorithm, the weight information is carried in Hello message. When the node receives its neighbor nodes' Hello messages, it updates the related nodes' reputation value. In addition, the node can update its degree and mobility, according to the number of Hello messages received and the transmission power, respectively. After receiving Hello message in some period, the node gets its initial weight. Then the node sends its weight through the broadcasted Hello message.

Compared with other nodes' weight, the node that has the highest weight is elected as cluster head. If the node A receives the cluster head message from its neighbor node B, and node B's reputation value is higher than A's, A will send the message to node B to join in its cluster. If node A hasn't received the cluster head's message during a period, it becomes an isolate cluster head which has no cluster member.

Cluster Update

Cluster update includes cluster rebuild and cluster healing. Although the cluster is established, the topology of the network still may change due to the mobility of node, the descending of the energy and other factors. Thus, the node may leave the original cluster, or the node may join in the cluster. The original cluster will not be effective. This is cluster reestablishment. In the cluster healing procedure, set the related threshold according the node's role, i.e., TCH, TGW and TCM ($TCH>TGW>TCM$) are the thresholds of cluster head, gateway and cluster member, respectively. When the node's reputation value is higher than its role's reputation threshold, it is suspicious. And then, if this node is cluster head or gateway, search its neighbor's reputation value. If it is higher than this suspicious node's, cancel the suspicious node's role of clusterhead, and elect this node as cluster head. Else, keep the suspicious node's role. If the suspicious node is cluster member, put it into the black list and isolate from the network.

2.9.   Applications of Clustering

Where clustering is being applied in various fields were some of the applications are:

Use of Clustering in Data Mining: Clustering is often one of the first steps in data mining analysis. It identifies groups of related records that can be used as a starting point for exploring further relationships. This technique supports the development of population segmentation models, such as demographic-based customer segmentation. Additional analyses using standard analytical and other data mining techniques can determine the characteristics of these segments with respect to some desired outcome. For example, the buying habits of multiple population segments might be compared to determine which segments to target for a new sales campaign. For example, a company those sales a variety of products may need to know about the sale of all of their products in order to check that what product is giving extensive sale and which is lacking. This is done by data mining techniques. But if the system clusters the products that are giving less sale then only the cluster of such products would have to be checked rather than comparing the sales value of all the products. This is actually to facilitate the mining process.

2.9.1. *Application of Clustering in Text Mining*

Text mining, also referred to as *text data mining*, roughly equivalent to *text analytics,* refers to the process of deriving high-quality information from text. High-quality information is typically derived through the devising of patterns and trends through means such as statistical pattern learning. Text mining usually involves the process of structuring the input text (usually parsing, along with the addition of some derived linguistic features and the removal of others, and subsequent insertion into a database), deriving patterns within the structured data, and finally evaluation and interpretation of the output. 'High quality' in text mining usually refers to some combination of relevance, novelty, and interestingness. Typical text mining tasks include text categorization, text clustering, concept/entity extraction, production of granular taxonomies, sentiment analysis, document summarization, and entity relation modeling Text mining consists of extraction information from hidden patterns in large text-data collections.

The query is given in the system were the given query is been founded by using the search navigation system. Where the documents based on query search is been given here in the diagram. Where is been extracted using name extractor. From the authorization list the ranking details are viewed on it.

2.9.2. *Working of Cluster in the Search Engines*

Where information retrieval system is works in the web documents on it. The document source is said to be the documents of the web page. The query is said to be the search engine. Using cluster the documents are classified based on the query in the information retrieval system. The ranked documents represent the relevant details present in the documents which are relevant to the search of the query. It is the mining of the data in the web page...in the database websites.

Some other Applications of Clustering

Where the clustering is being used in Fields of applications on it.

- Data Mining
- Pattern recognition
- Image analysis
- Bioinformatics
- Machine Learning
- Voice mining
- Image processing

- Text mining
- Web cluster engines
- Whether report analysis

2.10. Discussion

Cluster analysis is an unsupervised learning method that constitutes a cornerstone of an intelligent data analysis process [Emamian V et al., 2012]. Clustering criterion, this can be expressed via a cost function or some other type of rules. To take into account the type of clusters that are expected to occur in the data set. Hierarchical clustering techniques use various criteria to decide "locally" at each step which clusters should be joined (or split for divisive approaches). Clustering is a typical unsupervised learning technique for grouping similar data points. A clustering algorithm assigns a large number of data points to a smaller number of groups such that data points in the same group share the same properties while, in different groups, they are dissimilar.

Review Questions

1. Define cluster
2. Briefly explain the basic steps of cluster process.
3. What is Hierarchical Methods? Explain in detail.
4. List out the advantages of hierarchical clustering.
5. Explain about the partition clustering with example.
6. Discuss about the Model-based Clustering Methods in detail.
7. Elaborate the Clustering Algorithms for Ad Hoc Wireless Networks

CHAPTER III

DENSITY BASED CLUSTERING ALGORITHMS

3.1. Introduction

Numerous applications require the management of spatial data, i.e. data related to space. Spatial Database Systems *(SDBS)* (Gueting 1994) are database systems for the management of spatial data. Increasingly large amounts of data are obtained from satellite images, X-ray crystallography or other automatic equipment. Therefore, automated knowledge discovery becomes more and more important in spatial databases.

Several tasks of knowledge discovery in databases (KDD) have been defined in the literature [Matheus, Chan&P iatetsky-Shapiro 1993]. The task considered in this scheme is class identification, i.e. the group in go f the objects of a database into meaningful subclasses. In an earth observation database, e.g., it might want to discover classes of houses along some river. Clustering algorithms are attractive for the task of class identification.

However, the application to large spatial databases raises the following requirements for clustering algorithms:

- Minimal requirements of domain knowledge to determine the input parameters, because appropriate values are often not known in advance with large databases.
- Discovery of clusters with arbitrary shape, because the shape of clusters in spatial databases may be spherical, drawn-out, linear, elongated etc.
- Good efficiency on large databases, i.e. on databases of significantly more than just a few thousand objects. The well-known clustering algorithms offer no solution to the combination of these requirements. The new clustering algorithm DBSCAN. Requires only one input parameter and supports the user in deter mining an appropriate value for it. It discovers clusters of arbitrary shape. Finally, DBSCA is an efficient even for large spatial databases.

Outlier detection is an important topic in data analysis because of its applications to numerous domains. Density based clustering algorithms are capable of discovering clusters of arbitrary shapes and also this provides a natural protection against outliers [Patcha A and Park J. M, 2007]. Most partitioning method cluster objects based on the distance between objects. Such method can find only spherical shaped clusters and encounter difficulty in discovering clusters of arbitrary shape.

The general idea is to continue growing a given cluster as long as the density (the number of objects or data points) in the "neighborhood" exceeds a threshold. Such a method is able to filter out noises (outliers) and discover clusters of arbitrary shape. The density based clustering algorithms are considering normal clusters as dense regions of objects in the data space that are separated by regions of low density. Human normally identify a cluster because there is a relatively denser region compared to its sparse neighborhood. The representative density based clustering algorithms are DBSCAN, OPTICS and DENCLUE.

The DENCLUE algorithm employs a cluster model based on kernel density estimation and a cluster is density by a local maximum of the estimated density function. Data points are assigned to a cluster by hill climbing, i.e. points going to the same local maximum are put into the same cluster. The traditional density estimation algorithm considers only the location of the point, not variable of interest and hence hill climbing makes unnecessary small steps in the beginning and never converges exactly to the maximum. The hill climbing procedure for Gaussian kernels, which adjust the step size automatically. The DENCLUE algorithm does really converge towards a local maximum.

Clustering Algorithm

Clustering Algorithms There are two basic types of clustering algorithms (Kaufman & Rousseeuw 1990): partitioning and hierarchical algorithms. Partitioning algorithms construct a partition of a database of objects into a set of k clusters; k is an input parameter for these algorithms. The partitioning algorithm typically starts with an initial partition of D and then uses an iterative control strategy to optimize an objective function. Each cluster is represented by the gravity center of the cluster *(k-means algorithms)* or by one of the objects of the cluster located near its center *(k-medoid algorithms)*. Consequently, partitioning algorithms use a two-step procedure. First, determine k representatives minimizing the objective function. Second, assign each object to the cluster with its representative "closest" to the considered object. The second step implies that a partition is equivalent to a various diagram and each cluster is contained in one of the various cells. Thus, the shape of all clusters found by a partitioning algorithm is convex which is very restrictive.

Ng & Han (1994) explore partitioning algorithms for KDD in spatial databases. An algorithm called CLARANS (Clustering Large Applications based on Randomized Search) is introduced which is an improved k-medoid method. Compared to former k-medoid algorithms, CLARANS is more effective and more efficient. An experimental evaluation indicates that CLARArNuSns efficiently on databases of thousands of objects. Ng& Han (1 994) also discuss methods to determine the "natural" number knat of clusters in a database. They propose to run CLARAN on each k from 2 to n. For each of the discovered clustering the silhouette coefficient (Kaufman & Rousseeuw 1990) is calculated, and finally, the clustering with the maximum coefficient is chosen as the "natural" clustering. Unfortunately, the run time of this approach is prohibitive for large n, because it implies O (n) calls of CLARANS. CLARA hat all objects to be clustered can reside in main memory at the same time which does not hold for large databases. Furthermore, the run time of CLARANS is prohibitive on large databases. Therefore, Ester, Kriegel &Xu (1995) present several focusing techniques which address both of these problems by focusing the clustering process on the relevant parts of the database. First, the focus is small enough to be memory resident and second, the run time of Clarions the objects of the focus is significantly less than its run time on the whole database.

Hierarchical algorithms create a hierarchical decomposition of D. The hierarchical decomposition is represented by *a dendrogram*a, tree that iteratively splits D into smaller subsets until each subset consists of only one object. In such a hierarchy, each node of the tree represents a cluster of D. The algorithm can either be created from the leaves up to the root *(agglomerative approach)* or from the root down to the leaves *(divisive approach)* by merging or dividing clusters at each step. In contrast to partitioning algorithms, hierarchical algorithms do not need k as an input. However, termination condition has to be defined indicating when the merge or division process should be terminated. One example of a termination condition in the agglomerative approach is the critical distance between the clusters of Q. So far, the main problem with hierarchical clustering algorithms has been the difficulty of deriving appropriate parameters for the termination condition, e.g. a value of Dim which is small enough to separate all "natural" clusters and, at the same time large enough such that no cluster is split into two parts. Recently, in the area of signal processing the hierarchical algorithm Ej-cluster has been presented (Garcfa, Fdez-Valdivia, Cortijo & Molina 1994) automatically deriving a termination condition. Its key idea is that two points belong to the same cluster if you can walk from the first point to the second one by a "sufficiently small" step. Ej-cluster follows the divisive approach. It does not require any input of domain knowledge. Furthermore, experiments show that it is very effective in discovering non-convex clusters. However, the computational cost of Ej-cluster is O (n2) due to the -distance calculation for each pair of points. This is acceptable for applications such as character recognition with moderate values for n, but it is prohibitive for application on large databases. Jain (1988) explores a density based approach to identify clusters in k-dimensional point sets. The data set is partitioned into a number of no overlapping cells and histograms are constructed. Cells with relatively high frequency counts of points are the potential cluster centers and the boundaries between clusters fall in the "valleys" of the histogram. This method has the capability of identifying clusters of any shape. However, the space and run-time requirements for storing and searching multidimensional histograms can be enormous. Even if the space and run-time requirements are optimized, the performance of such an approach crucially depends on the size of the cells.

Distance Measure

An important step in most clustering is to select a distance measure, which will determine how the similarity of two elements is calculated. This will influence the shape of the clusters, as some elements may be close to one another according to one distance and farther away according to another. The 2-norm distance is the Euclidean distance, a generalization of the Pythagorean Theorem to more than two coordinates. It is what would be obtained if the distance between two points were measured with a ruler: the "intuitive" idea of distance. Based on this idea of finding the distance, the clustering qualities of the proposed algorithms are analyzed here.

3.2.   Density Based Clustering Algorithms

Clustering is a widely used unsupervised data mining technique. To discover clusters with arbitrary shape and outliers, density based clustering algorithm have been developed. Density based clustering is to discover clusters of arbitrary shape in databases with noise. It forms clusters based on maximal set of density connected points. The core part in density based clustering is density reach-ability and density connectivity. It requires two input parameters i.e. Eps which is known as radius and the MinPts i.e. the minimum number of points required to form a cluster. It starts with an arbitrary starting point that has not visited once. Then the ε neighborhood is retrieved and if it contains sufficiently many points than a cluster is started. Otherwise, the point is labeled as noise [Ester, M et al., 1996].

3.2.1. Density Based Connectivity Clustering

In this clustering technique density and connectivity both measured in terms of local distribution of nearest neighbors. So defined density connectivity is a symmetric relation and all the points reachable from core objects can be factorized into maximal connected components serving as clusters. The points that are not connected to any core point are declared to be outliers (they are not covered by any cluster). The non-core points inside a cluster represent its boundary. The core objects are internal points. Processing is independent of data ordering. So far, nothing requires any limitations on the dimension or attributes types.

3.2.2. Density Functions Clustering

In this density function is used to compute the density. Overall density is modeled as the sum of the density functions of all objects. Clusters are determined by density attractors, where density attractors are local maxima of the overall density function. The influence function can be an arbitrary one.

Density based clustering algorithms are DBSCAN (Density Based Spatial Clustering of Application with Noise), OPTICS (Ordering Points to Identify the Clustering Structure) and DENCLUE (DENsity based CLUtEring). DBSCAN grows clusters according to a density based connectivity analysis. OPTICS [Ankerst M.M et al., 1999] extends DBSCAN [Sander J.M et al., 1997; Chakraborty S and Nagwani N. K, 2011] to produce a cluster ordering obtained from a wide range of parameter settings. DENCLUE [Hinneburg A and Keim D.A, 1998] is a clustering analysis way based on a group of density distribution function, so can more formally define center-defined clusters and arbitrary shape ones.

In density based clustering, a cluster is defined as a connected dense component and grows in the direction driven by the density. Density based approaches apply a local cluster criterion [Jianhao Tan and Jing Zhang, 2010].

Clusters are regarded as regions in the data space in which the objects are dense and which are separated by regions of low object density (noise). These regions may have an arbitrary shape and the points inside a region may be arbitrarily distributed.

3.3. Density based Spatial Clustering of Application with Noise (DBSCAN)

DBSCAN is a data clustering algorithm and it is a density based clustering algorithm because it finds a number of clusters starting from the estimated density distribution of corresponding nodes. DBSCAN is one of the most common clustering algorithms and also most cited in scientific literature [Parimala M et al., 2011; Lu C et al., 2003].

DBSCAN definition of a cluster is based on the notion of density reach-ability.

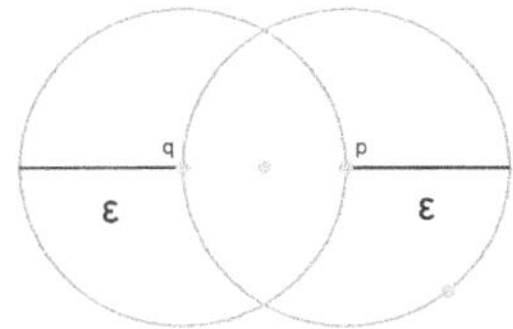

Fig. 3.1: Directly Density Reachable [Ram S et al., 2010]

In Fig 3.1 shows a point in an image q is directly density reachable from a point in an image p if it is not farther away than a given distance ε (i.e., is part of its ε-neighborhood) and if p is surrounded by sufficiently many points such that one may consider p and q to be part of a cluster. q is called density reachable ("directly density reachable") from p, if there is a sequence $p_1, p_2, ..., p_n$ of points with $p_1 = p_n$ and $p_n = q$ where each p_{i+1} is directly density reachable from p_i.

3.3.1. *DBSCAN Algorithm*

DBSCAN (Density Based Spatial Clustering of Applications with Noise) is of partitional type clustering where more dense regions are considered as cluster and low dense regions are called noise [Ester M et al., 1996].

Step 1: Pre-processing

First, a pre-processing step must be applied to the removal of noise and diffuse emission. As stated before, this might be accomplished by using a threshold.

Step 2: DBSCAN Clustering

Second, the DBSCAN algorithm can be applied on individual pixels to link together a complete emission area at the image for each channel of the electromagnetic spectrum. This is done by setting the Eps parameter to some value that will define the minimum area required for a source to be considered. The Eps parameter will define the distance metric in terms of pixels. Each of the generated clusters will define a celestial entity.

Step 3: Multi-spectral Correlation

After identifying all clusters, one can apply a multi spectral correlation process in order to consider the results (generated clusters) from every electromagnetic wavelength. A common approach would be only considering clusters which have one or more counterparts close enough with respect to some threshold on the other channels of the electromagnetic spectrum [Glory H. Shah et al., 2012].

3.3.2. *DBSCAN Algorithm Description*

The function DBSCAN ( ) is used to cluster the objects. It produces two vectors such as class and type.

The class vector is specifying assignment of the ith object to certain cluster (m, 1) and type vector is specifying type of the ith object (core: 1, border: 0, outlier: -1).

Function: [class, type] = Dbscan (x,k,Eps)

Aim: Clustering the data with Density Based Spatial Clustering of Application with   Noise (DBSCAN).

Input:

x   -   Data set (m,n); m-objects, n-variables.

MinPts   -   Number of objects in a neighborhood of an object.

(Minimal number of objects considered as a cluster).

Eps   -   Neighborhood radius, if not known avoid this parameter.

 Output:

Class   -   Vector specifying assignment of the ith object to certain cluster (m,1).

Type-   Vector specifying type of the ith object (core: 1, border: 0, outlier: -1).

DBSCAN requires two parameters: Epsilon (Eps) and Minimum Points (MinPts). It starts with an arbitrary starting point that has not been visited. It finds all the neighbor points within distance Eps of the starting point. If the number of neighbors is greater than or equal to MinPts, a cluster is formed. The starting point and its neighbors are added to this cluster and the starting point is marked as visited. The algorithm then repeats the evaluation process for all the neighbors' recursively. If the number of neighbors is less than MinPts, the point is marked as noise. If a cluster is fully expanded (all points within reach are visited) then the algorithm proceeds to iterate through the remaining unvisited points in the dataset.

3.4.   Ordering Points to Identify The Clustering Structure (OPTICS)

While the partitioning density based clustering algorithm DBSCAN can only identify a flat clustering, the newer algorithm OPTICS computes an ordering of the points augmented by additional information, i.e. the reach ability distance, representing the intrinsic hierarchical (nested) cluster structure [Ankerst M et al., 1999]. Ordering Points to Identify the Clustering Structure (OPTICS) is an algorithm for finding density based clusters in spatial data. The basic idea is similar to DBSCAN, but it addresses one of DBSCAN's major weaknesses, the problem of detecting meaningful clusters in data of varying density. In order to do so, the points of the database are linearly ordered such that points which are spatially closest become neighbors in the ordering. Additionally, a special distance is stored for each point that represents the density that needs to be accepted for a cluster in order to have both points belong to the same cluster [Anant Ram et al., 2010]. OPTICS generalizes clustering by creating an ordering of the points that allows the extraction of clusters with arbitrary values for ε. The OPTICS algorithm adopts the original DBSCAN algorithm to deal with variance density clusters. This algorithm computes an ordering of the objects based on the reach ability distance for representing the intrinsic hierarchical clustering structure. DBSCAN can cluster objects given input parameters such as ε and MinPts, it still leaves the user with the responsibility of selecting parameter values that will lead to the discovery of acceptable clusters.

Such parameter settings are usually empirically set and difficult to determine, especially for real world, high dimensional datasets. Most algorithms are very sensitive to such parameter values, slightly different settings may lead to very different clustering of the data. Moreover, high dimensional real datasets often have very skewed distributions, such that their intrinsic clustering structure may not be characterized by global density parameters. To help overcome this difficulty, a cluster analysis algorithm called OPTICS was proposed.

OPTICS computes an augmented cluster ordering for automatic and interactive cluster analysis. This ordering represents the density based clustering structure of the data. It contains information that is equivalent to density based clustering obtained from a wide range of parameter settings. The cluster ordering can be used to extract basic clustering information (such as cluster centers or arbitrary shaped clusters) as well as provide the intrinsic clustering structure.

DBSCAN, can easily see that for a constant MinPts value, density based clusters with respect to a higher density (i.e., a lower value for e) are completely contained in density connected sets obtained with respect to a lower density. Recall that the parameter ε is a distance it is the neighborhood radius. Therefore, in order to produce a set or ordering of density based clusters, can extend the DBSCAN algorithm to process a set of distance parameter values at the same time.

To construct the different clustering simultaneously, the objects should be processed in a specific order. This order selects an object that is density reachable with respect to the lowest ε value so that clusters with higher density will be finished. Based on this idea, two values need to be stored for each object core distance and reach ability distance [Akerst M et al., 1999]:

The **core distance** is the smallest distance ε, between p and an object in its ε neighborhood such that p would be a core object.

Core distance of an object p: Let p be an object from a database D, let ε be a distance value, let $N_\varepsilon(p)$ be the ε-neighborhood of p, let MinPts be a natural number and let MinPts-distance (p) be the distance from p to its MinPts' neighbor. Then, the core distance of p is defined as

Core distance$_{\varepsilon, \text{MinPts}}$(p) = UNDEFINED, if $(N_\varepsilon(p)) <$ MinPts

MinPts-distance (p), otherwise

The core-distance of an object p is simply the smallest distance ε between p and an object in its ε-neighborhood such that p would be a core object with respect to ε, if this neighbor is contained in $N_ε(p)$. Otherwise, the core distance is UNDEFINED [Akerst M et al., 1999].

The **reach-ability distance** of p is the smallest distance such that p is density reachable from a core object o.Reach-ability distance object p with respect to object o: Let p and o be objects from a database *D*, let $N_ε(o)$ be the ε-neighborhood of o, and let MinPts be a natural number. Then, the reach ability distance of p with respect to o is defined as

Reach-ability distance$_{ε,MinPts}$(p, o) =UNDEFINED, if $N_ε(o)$ < MinPts

max (coredistance(o), distance(o, p)),otherwise.

The reach-ability distance of an object p with respect to another object o is the smallest distance such that p is directly density reachable from o if o is a core object. In this case, the reach-ability distance cannot be smaller than the core distance of o because for smaller distances no object is directly density reachable from o. Otherwise, if o is not a core object, even at the generating distance ε, the reach-ability distance of p with respect to o is UNDEFINED. The reach-ability distance of an object p depends on the core object with respect to which it is calculated. The generating distance ε is the largest distance considered for clusters. Clusters can be extracted for all $ε_i$ such that $0 ≤ ε_i ≤ ε$.

3.4.1. *OPTICS Algorithm*

Step 1: Find core distance of an object p is the smallest ε value that makes {p} a core object. If p is not core object, the core distance of p is undefined

Step 2: The reach-ability distance of an object q with respect to another object p is the greater value of   the core distance of p and the Euclidean distance between p and q. If p is not a core object, the reach-ability distance between p and q is undefined [Glory H. Shah et al., 2012; Mahmoud E et al., 2012].

Table 3.1: OPTICS Using ε= 1.2 and MinPts=2 and Distance type=Euclidian

No. Of Samples	270	452	3196	5000	7485
No of Clusters formed	0	0	0	0	0
No of Unclustered	270	452	3196	5000	7485
Instance noise level	Very Low	Very Low	Very High	No	Very High
Taken(Min.Sec)	0.06	3.31	18.64	301.16	7365.66

The Table 3.1 describes the OPTICS has more ability than DBSCAN to handle noise as DBSCAN is generating more clusters [Glory H. Shah et al., 2012] and includes number of clusters formed, and time taken to form a cluster, unclustered instances as well as the content of noise found. Noise Ratio which can have either of the values i.e. high, very high, less, very less, no noise and almost negligible means there is noise but only some percent and time taken when distance is changed.

3.4.2. OPTICS Algorithm Description

Function: [RD,CD,order]=optics(x,k)

Aim   :

Ordering objects of a data set to obtain the clustering structure

Input   :

x   -   Data set (m,n); m-objects, n-variables.

k   -   Number of objects in a neighborhood of the selected object.

(Minimal number of objects considered as a cluster)

Output   :

Reach-ability distance [RD]   - vector with reach ability distances (m, 1).

Core Distance [CD]   - vector with core distances (m, 1).

Order   - vector specifying the order of objects (1, m).

3.4.3. OPTICS Complexity

OPTICS is superior to DBSCAN. OPTICS is having least run time compared to DBSCAN. DBSCAN run time is nearly equal to three times the run time of OPTICS. The complexity of OPTICS is O (n^2). Because OPTICS is an extension of DBSCAN and equivalent with DBSCAN in structure, they have the same time complexity. OPTICS can realize auto and alternative clustering and is not sensitive to parameters. So slow running speed is one of its drawbacks [Ankerst M et al., 1999].

3.5.   Density Based Clustering (DENCLUE)

The DENCLUE [Hinneburg A and Keim D.A, 2003] builds on non-parametric methods, namely kernel density estimation. Non-parametric methods are not looking for optimal parameters of some model, but estimate desired quantities like the probability density of the data directly from the data instances. This allows a more direct definition of a clustering in contrast to parametric methods, where a clustering corresponds to an optimal parameter setting of some high dimensional function. A clustering in the DENCLUE is defined by the local maxima of the estimated density function. A hill-climbing procedure is started for each data instance, which assigns the instance to local maximum. The hill climbing procedure starts at a data point and iterates until the density does not grow anymore. A practical problem of gradient based hill climbing in general is the adaptation of the step size.

Hinneburg A and Keim D.A [1998] suggested DENCLUE from the basis of good development in statistics and pattern recognition, well-known as "kernel density estimation". The two parameters supported the performance of the data clustering including the σ and ε. The σ parameter was the determiner of the effect of the proximal point, it had influence on the proximal point and the amount of intervening data. Meanwhile, the ε parameter contained the lowest density amongst the density attractor.

The density based clustering algorithm described kernel density estimation. The main goal of density estimation is to find the dense regions of points, which is essentially the same as clustering. Kernel density estimation is a non-parametric technique that does not assume any fixed probability model of the clusters, as in the case of K-means or model-based clustering via the EM algorithm. Instead, kernel density estimation tries to infer the underlying probability density at each point in the dataset [Jianhao Tan and Jing Zhang, 2010].

DENCLUE (DENsity-based CLUstEring) [Zhou S et al., 2003] is a clustering algorithm based on a set of density distribution functions. The DENCLUE [Hinneburg A and Keim D. A., 2003] builds on non-parametric methods, namely kernel density estimation. Non-parametric methods are not looking for optimal parameters of some model, but estimate desired quantities like the probability density of the data directly from the data instances. This allows a more direct definition of a clustering in contrast to parametric methods, where a clustering corresponds to an optimal parameter setting of some high dimensional function.

In the DENCLUE, the probability density in the data space is estimated as a function of all data instances. A clustering in the DENCLUE is defined by the local maxima of the estimated density function. A hill-climbing procedure is started for each data instance, which assigns the instance to local maxima. The hill climbing procedure starts at a data point and iterates until the density does not grow anymore. The problem of gradient based hill climbing in general is the adaptation of the step size [Parimala M et al., 2011].

The algorithm is built on the following ideas:

- The influence of each data point can be formally modeled using a mathematical function, called an influence function, which describes the impact of a data point within its neighborhood.
- The overall density of the data space can be modeled analytically as the sum of the influence function applied to all data points.
- Clusters can then be determined mathematically by identifying density attractors, where density attractors or local maxima of the overall density function.

By density function, the gradient and density attractor of the function can be defined [Peter H and Antonysamy, 2010; Zhou S et al., 2003]. A point is density attracted by a density attractor if there are a group of points $x_0,x_1,...,x_k,x_0=x$, $x_k=x^*$ for $0<i<k$ the gradient of x_{i+1} is along x_i. For a continuous differential influence function, density attractors of a group of data points can be calculated with the help of the hill climbing algorithm using the gradient.

Based on these concepts, the center-defined cluster and arbitrary-shape one can be formally defined. The center-defined cluster of a density attractor x^* is a subset c density abstracted by x^*, whose density function value is no less than the threshold ε, Otherwise, namely, if its density function value is less than the threshold ε, it is called an isolated point.

An arbitrary-shape cluster is a set of the subset c. From one area to another, there exists a path, along which the density function value of each point is no less than ε. DENCLUE also generalizes other clustering methods such as density based clustering, partition based clustering, hierarchical clustering. In density based clustering DBSCAN is the example and square wave influence function is used and multicenter defined clusters are used two parameter σ = Eps, ε = MinPts.

Table 3.2: Comparisons of DBSCAN, OPTICS and DENCLUE [Glory H et al., 2012]

Name	DBSCAN	OPTICS	DENCLUE
Noise	Yes	Yes	Yes
Varied Density	No	Yes	Yes
Primary Input Required	Cluster radius, Minimum no. of Objects	Density Threshold	Radius
Complexity	$O(n \log n)$	$O(n \log n)$	$O(n^2)$
Data Type	Numerical	Numerical	Numerical
Cluster Type	arbitrary	Arbitrary	arbitrary
Data Set	High Dimensional	High Dimensional	High Dimensional

In Table 3.2 shows that run time of DENCLUE algorithm is lowest compared to the existing algorithm. DENCLUE produces good clustering results even when a large amount of noise is present. As in most other approaches, the quality of the resulting clustering depends on an adequate choice of the parameters. In this approach, the two important parameters are used, namely σ and ε. The parameter σ determines the influence of an object in its neighborhood and ε describes whether a density attractor is significant. Density attractors are local maxima of the overall density function. The computational complexity of the algorithm is O (n log n). Where n is the number of objects to be clustered.

3.6. Influence Function and Density Function

An improved DENCLUE algorithm is based on the idea that the influence of each data point can be modeled using a mathematical function called influence function. The influence function can be seen as a function which describes the impact of a data point within its neighborhood. Examples for influence functions are parabolic functions, square wave function or Gaussian functions and the influence function is applied to each data point.

The overall density of the data space is calculated as the sum of the influence function of all data points. Clusters are determined by identifying density attractors. Density attractors are local maxima of the overall density function. If the overall density function is continuous and differentiable at any point, determining the density attractors can be done efficiently by a local maximum. In addition, the overall density function allows clusters of arbitrary shape to be described in a very compact form, namely by a simple equation of the overall density function and also shows that method is invariant against large amounts of noise and works well for high dimensional data sets.

The overall density function requires summing up the influence functions of all data points. Most of the data points, however, do not actually contribute to the overall density function. Therefore, DENCLUE uses a local density function which considers only the data points which actually contribute to the overall density function. An intelligent cell based organization of the data allows the algorithm to work efficiently on very large amounts of high dimensional data.

3.6.1. Influence Function

The influence function can be arbitrary set and it can be defined on the basis of the distance measures. Each data points in an image can be calculated using the Euclidean distance function $d((x_1, y_1), (x_2, y_2))$ where $d(x, y)$ is the distance between x and y.

Step 1:	Find the distance of dataset1 (x) and dataset2 (y).
Step 2:	Find I(x, y) = exp {- (distance(x, y) **2) / (2*(sigma**2))}

Fig. 3.2: Algorithm for Influence Function

Let x and y be objects or points of dataset1 and dataset2. The influence of each data point can be calculated as a function and the function is called influence function. Influence function describes the impact of data point within its neighborhoods. It can be used to compute a Gaussian influence function.

3.6.2. *Density Function*

The density function at an object or point in an image is defined as the sum of influence functions of all data points.

Step 1:	Repeat the steps influence function until end of the data set to find sum of influence of each another dataset.
Step 2:	Density = Density + Influence (entity, sigma).

Fig. 3.3: Algorithm for Density Function

The density function at an object or point x is defined as the sum of influence functions of all data points. That is, it is the total influence on x of all of the data points. From the density function can define the density attractor, the local maxima of the overall density function. A hill climbing algorithm guided by the gradient can be used to determine the density attractor of a set of data points. The gradient of the density function start from x and climb along the direction of the gradient of its density function and reached the local maxima of the density function or density attractor.

3.7. Local Maximum Procedure

The density of an object is greater than its surrounding object and the object is called density attractor or local maximum. Objects that are associated with same density attractor belong to same cluster.

Step 1:	Take arbitrary any object x_i.
Step 2:	Repeat step3 until find local density attractor (x_n < density threshold).
Step 3:	Calculate gradient to find neighbor point.
Step 4:	Move to next point x_{i+1}.

Fig. 3.4: Algorithm for Density Attractor

The basic idea of hill climbing strategy, Stochastically choose a data as current data, climb the hill of density function with a step length, search the next data along its gradient direction and compare density values of current data and next data, if the density value of next data is larger, then replaces the next data as new current data and continue searches the next data with the step length along gradient direction until the density value of next data is smaller than current data. If density value of current data is larger than threshold, then all those data visited by hill climbing are in one cluster, else those data are outliers.

3.8. Clustering and Outlier Detection

Outlier detection aims to detect changes in an image over time (motion detection) or in regions which appear abnormal on the image. This domain includes satellite imagery, digit recognition, spectroscopy, mammographic image and video surveillance. The outliers are caused by motion or insertion of foreign object or instrumentation errors. The data has spatial as well as temporal characteristics. Each data point has a few continuous attributes such as color, lightness, texture, etc. The interesting outliers are either anomalous points or regions in the images (point and contextual outliers). The proposed Denclue method group the objects based the location and variable of interest.

Step 1: Data Set O ={ o_1, o_2, o_3, o_4, ... o_n},

Step 2: Find (Highly) Populated Cells

(Use a threshold=ε_c)

Step 3: Identify populated cells (use location and variable of interest).

Step 4: For any uncluster data objects, find density attractor points, C*, using hill climbing iteratively:

(i) Randomly pick a point, p_i.

(ii) Compute local density (r=4σ). (σ, the standard deviation).

(iii) Pick another point, p_{i+1}, close to p_i, compute local density at p_{i+1}.

(iv) If LocDen(p_i) < LocDen(p_{i+1}), climb.

(v) Put all points within distance $\sigma/2$ of path, p_i, p_{i+1} ...C*

Step 5: Connect the density attractor clusters into a density attractor cluster called C*, using a threshold ε, on the local densities of the attractors.

Step 6: If any object does not belongs to C* then it is outlier.

Fig. 3.5: Algorithm for Clustering and Outlier Detection

In Fig3.4 shows the proposed DENCLUE algorithm. The dataset O contain the number of objects. To group the object based on location and variable of interest. Based on these criteria the numbers of clusters are reduced and the exact outlier objects are mined in an effective manner.

3.9. Density based Clustering Algorithms for Very Large Datasets

Due to this the large amount of text are usually uploaded into many sites and thus it need to be classified. Data mining is the process of extracting useful information from databases. Many approaches to temporal data mining have been proposed to extract useful information, such as time series analysis, temporal association rules mining, and sequential pattern discovery. Several core techniques that are used in data mining describe the type of mining and data recovery operation.

Clustering is still an important research issue in the data mining, because there is a continuous research in data mining for optimum clusters on spatial data. There are various types of partition based and hierarchal algorithms implemented for clustering and the clusters which are formed based on the density are easy to understand and it does not limit itself to certain shapes of the clusters. Density-based clustering methods try to find clusters based on the density of points in regions. Intense or dense regions that are accessible from each other are merged to produce clusters. Density-based clustering methods surpass at finding clusters of arbitrary shapes.

A spatial database system is a database system for the management of spatial data. Speedy growth is happening in the number and the size of spatial databases for applications such as traffic control, geo-marketing, and environmental reviews. Spatial data mining or knowledge discovery in spatial databases links to the mining from spatial databases of contained knowledge, spatial relations, or extra patterns that are not unambiguously store.

Clustering schemes are classified as hierarchical partitioning, density-based, grid-based and mixed methods. Partitioning methods are the most popular clustering algorithms. The advantage of partitioning approaches is fast clustering, while the disadvantages are the instability of the clustering result, and inability to filter noise data. Hierarchical methods involve constructing a hierarchical tree structure, and adopting it to perform clustering. These methods have high clustering accuracy, but suffer from continuously repetitive merging and partitioning: each instance must compare the attribute of all objects, leading to a high calculation complexity. Density-based methods perform clustering based on density. These approaches can filter noise, and perform clustering in tangled patterns, but take a long time to execute clustering. Grid-based clustering algorithms segment data space into various grids, where each data point falls into a grid, and perform clustering with the data points inside the grids, thus significantly reducing the clustering time.

Spatial clustering goals to group alike objects into the same group based on considering both spatial and non-spatial attributes of the object and a regular clustering algorithm can be modified to account for the special nature of spatial data to give a spatial clustering algorithm.

Spatial Data Mining

Clustering is still an important research issue in the data mining, because there is a continuous research in data mining for optimum clusters on spatial data. There are numerous types of partition based and hierarchal algorithms implemented for clustering and the clusters which are formed based on the density are easy to understand and it does not limit itself to certain shapes of the clusters.

Spatial data mining is the branch of data mining that deals with spatial (location, or geo-referenced) data. The knowledge tasks involving spatial data include finding characteristic rules, discriminate rules, association rules; etc. A spatial characteristic rule is a general description of spatial data. A spatial discriminate rule is a common explanation of the features discriminating or contrasting a class of spatial data from other class. Spatial association rules describe the association among objects, derived from spatial neighborhood relations. It can associate spatial attributes with spatial attributes, or spatial attributes with non-spatial attributes.

3.10. K-Means Clustering

K-Means Clustering is a method of cluster analysis which aims to partition n observations into k clusters in which each observation belongs to the cluster with the nearest mean. The algorithm is called *k-means,* where k represents the number of clusters required, since a case is allocated to the cluster for which its distance to the cluster mean is the negligible. The achievement in the algorithm centres on finding the *k-means.*

Hierarchical Clustering builds a cluster hierarchy or a tree of clusters, it is also known as a „dendrogram". All cluster nodes contains child clusters; sibling clusters partition the points covered by their common parent.

DBSCAN finds all clusters properly, independent of the shape, size, and location of clusters to everyone, and is greater to a widely used Clarans method. DBscan is based on two main concepts: density reach ability and density connect ability. These both concepts depend on two input parameters of the DBSCAN clustering: the size of epsilon neighbourhood e and the minimum points in a cluster m. The number of point"s parameter impacts detection of outliers. Points are declared to be outliers if there are few other points in the e-Euclidean neighbourhood. e parameter controls the size of the neighbourhood, as well as the size of the clusters. The Euclidean space has an open set that can be divided into a set of its connected components. The execution of this idea for partitioning of a finite set of points requires concepts of density, connectivity and boundary.

OPTICS ("Ordering Points to Identify the Clustering Structure") is an algorithm for finding density-based clusters in spatial data. Its fundamental idea is comparable to DBSCAN, but it addresses one of DBSCAN's main weaknesses: the problem of detecting significant clusters in data of changeable density. Consecutively the points of the database are linearly ordered such that points that are spatially closest become neighbours in the ordering. Furthermore, a special distance is stored for each point that corresponds to the density that needs to be accepted for a cluster in order to have both points belong to the same cluster.

SOFT DBSCAN: Soft DBSCAN is a very much recent clustering techniques. This technique combines DBSCAN and fuzzy set theory. The idea is to improve the clusters generated by DBSCAN by fuzzy set theory which is based on an objective function, in order to produce optimal fuzzy partitions. This new method could provide a similar result as Fuzzy C Means, but it is simple and superior in handling outlier points. Thusly, the Soft DBSCAN"s first stage runs DBSCAN which creates, many seed clusters, with a bunch of noisy points. Each noisy is consider as one cluster. These determined groups, in addition of noisy clusters, with their centers, offer a good estimate for initial degrees of membership which express proximities of data entities to the cluster centers. This update the membership values in every iteration since these last ones depend on the new cluster centers. When the cluster center stabilizes "soft DBSCAN" algorithm stops.

Fuzzy Set Theory: The notion of a fuzzy set provides a convenient point of departure for the construction of a conceptual framework which parallels in many respects the framework used in the case of ordinary sets, but is more general than the latter and, potentially, may prove to have a much wider scope of applicability, particularly in the fields of pattern classification and information processing. Fuzzy set theory provides a strict mathematical framework (there is nothing fuzzy about fuzzy set theory!) in which vague conceptual phenomena can be precisely and rigorously studied. It can also be considered as a modeling language, well suited for situations in which fuzzy relations, criteria, and phenomena exist. Fuzzy Logic can be applied to a Decision Tree to generate a Fuzzy Rule-Based System. This is particularly useful when at least some of the attributes that are tested in the decision nodes are numerical. In this case, the tests can be formulated using labels (e.g., "if Temperature is low") and the children nodes will be partially activated.

3.11. Related on Density Based Clustering

Xin Wang and Howard J. Hamilton presented A Comparative Study of Two Density-Based Spatial Clustering Algorithms for Very Large Datasets. They compare two spatial clustering methods. DBSCAN gives extremely good results and is efficient in many datasets. However, if a dataset has clusters of widely changeable densities, DBSCAN is unable to handle it proficiently. If non-spatial attributes play a role in determining the desired clustering result, DBSCAN is not appropriate, because it does not consider non-spatial attributes in the dataset. DBRS aims to reduce the running time for datasets with varying densities. It scales well on high-density clusters. DBRS can be deal with a property associated to non-spatial attribute(s) through a purity threshold, when finding the matching neighborhood. One limitation of the algorithm is that it sometimes may fail to combine some small clusters.

Cheng-Fa Tsai and Chun-Yi Sung proposed DBSCALE: An Efficient Density-Based Clustering Algorithm for Data Mining in Large Databases. They present a novel clustering algorithm that incorporates neighbour searching and expansion seed selection into a density-based clustering algorithm. Data Points have been clustered require not be input again when searching for neighborhood data points and the algorithm redefines eight Marked Boundary Objects to add expansion seeds according to far centrifugal force that increases coverage. Investigational results point out that the proposed DBSCALE has a lower execution time cost than KIDBSCAN, MBSCAN and DBSCAN clustering algorithms. DBSCALE has a highest divergence in clustering accuracy rate of 0.29'Yo, and a maximum deviation in noise data clustering rate of 0.14%.

DBSCAN Algorithm proposed by Ester et al. in 1996, was the first clustering algorithm to employ density as a condition. It utilizes density clustering to place data points into the same cluster when their density within their data points is higher than a set threshold value, and sets this cluster as the seed for outward expansion. This algorithm must set two parameters, the radius (e) and the minimum number of included points (MinPts). DBSCAN can conduct clustering on disordered patterns, and has noise filtering capacity, as well as clusters that can be stabilized.

K. Ganga Swathi and KNVSSK Rajesh proposed Comparative analysis of clustering of spatial databases with various DBSCAN Algorithms. They present the comparative analysis of the various density based clustering mechanisms. There is certain problem on existing density based algorithms because they are not capable of finding the meaningful clusters whenever the density is so much different. VDBSCAN is commenced to compensate this problem. It is same as DBSCAN (Density Based Spatial Clustering of Applications with Noise) but only the difference is VDBSCAN selects several values of parameter Eps for different densities according to k-dist plot. The difficulty is the significance of parameter k in k-dist plot is user defined. This introduces a new technique to find out the value of parameter k automatically based on the characteristics of the datasets. In this method they consider spatial distance from a point to all others points in the datasets. The clustering algorithm is based on density approach and can detect global as well as embedded clusters. Investigational outputs are reported to establish the superiority of the algorithm in light of several synthetic data sets. In this they considered two-dimensional objects. But, spatial databases also contain extended objects such as polygons. Due to that, there is possibility for scaling the proposed algorithm to detect clusters in such datasets with minor alterations, research is in progress. From a proper analysis of the intended technique, it can be securely concluded that the algorithm implemented is working appropriately to a great extent.

DBSCAN algorithm is based on center-based approach, one of definitions of density. In the center-based approach, density is estimated for a particular point in the dataset by counting the number of points within a particular radius, *Eps*, of that point. This contains the point itself. The center-based approach to density tolerates to classify a point as a core point, a noise, a border point and background point. A point called core point if the numerous points inside *Eps*, a user-specified parameter, surpass a certain threshold, *MinPts*, which is a user-specified parameter.

Pragati Shrivastava and Hitesh Gupta present a review of Density-Based clustering in Spatial Data. Spatial data mining is the branch of data mining that deals with spatial (location, or geo-referenced) data. The knowledge tasks involving spatial data include finding characteristic rules, discriminate rules, association rules; etc. A spatial characteristic rule is a general description of spatial data. A spatial distinguish rule is a universal description of the features discriminating or contrasting a class of spatial data from other class. Spatial association rules describe the association between objects, based on spatial neighbourhood relations. They can associate spatial attributes with spatial attributes, or spatial attributes with non-spatial attributes. They represent the density based clustering. That is uses to reduced core points, outliers and noise. When reduces this points than increase the efficiency of clustering. Core points are basically related to the centres at any single tone problem and noise is the combination of outlier and core point.

Manish Verma et al., proposed A Comparative Study of Various Clustering Algorithms in Data Mining. They provide a comparative study among various clustering. They compared six types of clustering techniques- k-Means Clustering, Optics, DBScan clustering, Hierarchical Clustering, Density Based Clustering and EM Algorithm. These clustering techniques are implemented and analyzed using a clustering tool WEKA. Performances of the 6 techniques are presented and compared. Running the clustering algorithm using any software produces almost the same result even when changing any of the factors because most of the clustering software uses the same procedure in implementing any algorithm.

Abir, and Eloudi presented Soft DBSCAN: Improving DBSCAN Clustering method using fuzzy set theory. They propose a novel clustering algorithm called "Soft DBSCAN" which is inspired by FCM algorithm. Much of the strength of this approach comes from FCM"s ideas. The plan of "soft DBSCAN" is to make the DBSCANs clusters robust, extending them with the fuzzy set theory. DBSCAN is run in the first phase to produce a set of clusters with diverse shapes and sizes, in the company of noisy data discrimination. In the second phase, it computes the degrees of fuzzy membership which express proximities of data entities to the cluster centers.

They suggested method does not only outperform FCM clustering by detecting points expected to be noises and handling the arbitrary shape, but also by generating more dense clusters. Evaluations demonstrate that the solution generates more accurate groups for input dataset and objective function is improved better than FCM. In year 2012, Xiaojun LOU, Junying LI, and Haitao LIU proposed a technique to Improved Fuzzy C-means Clustering Algorithm Based on Cluster Density.

They study on the distribution of the data set, and introduce a definition of cluster density as the representation of the inherent character of the data set. A regulatory factor based on cluster density is proposed to correct the distance measure in the conventional FCM. It differs from other approaches in that the regulator uses both the shape of the data set and the middle result of iteration operation. And the distance measure function is dynamically corrected by the regulatory factor until the objective criterion is achieved. Two sets of experiments using artificial data and UCI data are operated. Comparing with some existing methods, the proposed algorithm shows the better performance. The experiment results reveal that FCM-CD has a good tolerance to different densities and various cluster shapes. And FCM-CD shows a higher performance in clustering accuracy.

Andrew McCallum et al offered Efficient Clustering of High Dimensional Data Sets with Application to Reference Matching. have focused on reference matching, a particular class of problems that arise when one has many different descriptions for each of many different objects, and wishes to know (1) which descriptions refer to the same object, and (2) what the best description of that object is. They present experimental results for the domain of bibliographic reference matching. Another significant illustration of this class is the merge-purge problem. Companies often purchase and merge multiple mailing lists. The resulting list then has multiple entries for each household. Even for a single person, the name and address in each version on the list may diverge slightly, with middle initials absent or present, words shortened or expanded, zip codes present or absent. This problem of merging large mailing lists and eliminating duplicates becomes even more complex for householding, where one wishes to collapse the records of multiple people who live in the same household.

Hrishav Bakul Barua et al., offered a "Density Based Clustering Technique" for Large Spatial Data Using Polygon Approach. The technique of data clustering has been inspected, which is a particular type of data mining problem. The procedure of grouping a set of physical or abstract objects into classes of similar objects is called clustering. The objective of this algorithm is to present a Triangle-density based clustering technique, which named as TDCT, for efficient clustering of spatial data. This algorithm is accomplished of recognizing embedded clusters of arbitrary shapes as well as multi-density clusters over large spatial datasets. The Polygon approach is being accessed to execute the clustering where the number of points inside a triangle (triangle density) of a polygon is calculated using barycentre formula.

This is because of the information that partitioning of the data set can be performed more efficiently in triangular shape than in any other polygonal shape due to its smaller space dimension. The ratio of numerous points among two triangles can be found out which forms the basis of nested clustering.

Chaudhari Chaitali G. Optimizing Clustering Technique based on Partitioning DBSCAN and Ant Clustering Algorithm, Clustering is the process of organizing similar objects into the same clusters and dissimilar objects in to dissimilar cluster. Correspondences between objects are estimated by using the attribute value of object; a distance metric is used for evaluating difference. DBSCAN algorithm is striking because it can find arbitrary shaped clusters with noisy outlier and require only two input parameters. DBSCAN algorithm is very successful for analyzing huge and complex spatial databases. DBSCAN necessitate bulky volume of memory support and has complexity with high dimensional data. Partitioning-based DBSCAN was suggesting overcoming these problems. But DBSCAN and PDBSCAN algorithms are responsive to the initial parameters. Author present a new algorithm based on partitioning-based DBSCAN and Ant-clustering. This algorithm can partition database in to N partitions according to the density of data. New PACA-DBSCAN algorithm reduces the sensitivity to the initial parameters and also can deal with data of uneven density. This algorithm does not need to discuss the distribution of data on each dimension for multidimensional data. PACA-DBSCAN algorithm can cluster data of very special shape. To evaluate the performance of proposed algorithm they use three dataset to compare with other algorithms.

Glory H. Shah et al., proposed An Empirical Evaluation of Density-Based Clustering Techniques. Conventional database querying methods are inadequate to extract useful information from massive data banks. Cluster investigation is one of the most important data analysis methods. It is the ability of detecting groups of comparable objects in bulky data sets without having specified groups by means of unambiguous features. The difficulty of detecting clusters of points is challenging when the clusters are of unusual size, density and shape. The expansion of clustering algorithms has received a lot of attention in the last few years and many new clustering algorithms have been proposed.

Santosh Kumar Rai and Nishchol Mishra DBCSVM: Density Based Clustering Using Support Vector Machines. They present an improved DBSCAN clustering algorithm named DBCSVM: Density Based Clustering Using Support Vector Machines. In the process of feature extraction generator, huge amount of matrix for the calculation of description of feature for the purpose of clustering, for this purpose previous density based clustering take more time and does not give better result. From this method the separation of farer and nearer points are very efficient. The farer points jumps into the next step of clustering. This method gives better result and takes less time comparison to previous DBSCAN clustering methods.

3.12. K Means Algorithm

The naive k-means algorithm partitions the dataset into 'k' subsets such that all records, from now on referred to as points, in a given subset "belong" to the same center. Also the points in a given subset are closer to that center than to any other center. The algorithm keeps track of the centroids of the subsets, and proceeds in simple iterations. The initial partitioning is randomly generated, that is, randomly initialize the centroids to some points in the region of the space. In each iteration step, a new set of centroids is generated using the existing set of centroids following two very simple steps. Let us denote the set of centroids after the ith iteration by C(i).

Problems with k-means Clustering Algorithm

The algorithm is simple and has nice convergence but there are number of problems with this. Some of the weaknesses of k-means are:

- When the numbers of data are not so many, initial grouping will determine the cluster significantly.
- The result is circular cluster shape because based on distance.
- The number of cluster, K, must be determined beforehand. Selection of value of K is itself an issue and sometimes it's hard to predict beforehand the number of clusters that would be there in data.
- Never know the real cluster, using the same data, if it is inputted in a different order may produce different cluster if the number of data is few.
- Sensitive to initial condition. Different initial condition may produce different result of cluster. The algorithm may be trapped in the local optimum.
- Never know which attribute contributes more to the grouping process since assume that each attribute has the same weight.
- Weakness of arithmetic mean is not robust to outliers. Very far data from the centroid may pull the centroid away from the real one.
- Experiments have shown that outliers can be a problem and can force algorithm to identify false clusters.

3.13. K-Means

K-mean algorithm is one of the centroid based technique. It takes input parameter k and partition a set of n object from k cluster. The similarity between clusters is measured in regards to the mean value of the object. The random selection of k object is first step of algorithm which represents cluster mean or center. By comparing most similarity other objects are assigning to the cluster.

Input: K: the number of clusters

D: a data set containing n object

Output: A set of k clusters

Method: step1: select K points as the initial centroids step2: repeat step3: From K clusters by assigning all points to the closest centroid step4: Re compute the centroid of each cluster. step5: Until the centroids don't change.

K-Medoids The k-means method is based on the centroid techniques to represent the cluster and it is sensitive to outliers. This means, a data object with an extremely large value may disrupt the distribution of data. To overcome the problem used K-medoids method which is based on representative object techniques. Medoid is replaced with centroid to represent the cluster. Medoid is the most centrally located data object in a cluster. Here, k data objects are selected randomly as medoids to represent k cluster and remaining all data objects are placed in a cluster having medoid nearest (or most similar) to that data object. After processing all data objects, new medoid is determined which can represent cluster in a better way and the entire process is repeated. Again all data objects are bound to the clusters based on the new medoids. In each iteration, medoids change their location step by step. This process is continued until no any medoid move. As a result, k clusters are found representing a set of n data objects. An algorithm for this method is given below.

Algorithm: PAM, a k-medoids algorithm for partitioning based on medoid or central objects.

Input:

- K: the number of clusters,
- D: a data set containing n objects.

Outputs:

- A set of k clusters.

Method:

a) Arbitrarily choose k objects in D as the initial representative objects or seeds;

b) Repeat

c) Assign each remaining object to the cluster with the nearest representative object;

d) Randomly select a non-representative object, Orandom.

e) Compute the total cost of swapping representative object, Oj with Orandom;

f) If S<0 then swap Oj with Orandom to form the new set of k representative object;

g) Until no change;

3.14. Discussion

Density based clustering ways provide a way of solving the clustering of arbitrary shape datasets. There are such typical algorithms as DBSCAN, OPTICS and DENCLUE among density based clustering methods. DBSCAN divides districts with enough high density into clusters and can detect arbitrary shape clusters in space databases with noises. But the algorithm asks users determine input parameters according to their experiences, which is not very available toward real high dimensional datasets. In addition, the algorithm is much sensitive to parameter values, whose tiny changes can produce clustering results with great differences.

OPTICS calculates a clustering ordering for auto and alternative clustering analysis and the ordering represents the density based clustering structure of data, which includes this information equal to density based clustering required from a clustering required from a comprehensive parameter set scope. OPTICS is superior to DBSCAN. OPTICS is having least run time compared to DBSCAN. DBSCAN run time is nearly equal to three times the run time of OPTICS. The complexity of OPTICS is O (n^2). Because OPTICS is an extension of DBSCAN and equivalent with DBSCAN in structure, they have the same time complexity. OPTICS can realize auto and alternative clustering and is not sensitive to parameters. So slow running speed is one of its drawbacks.

In the DENCLUE, the probability density in the data space is estimated as a function of all data instances. A clustering in the DENCLUE is defined by the local maxima of the estimated density function. A hill-climbing procedure is started for each data instance, which assigns the instance to local maxima. The hill climbing procedure starts at a data point and iterates until the density does not grow anymore. The execution of the DENCLUE is faster than DBSCAN and OPTICS but in terms of cluster quality DENCLUE is lacking behind. So, the proposed DENCLUE algorithm is improved and formulated for cluster quality.

Review Questions

1. What is knowledge discovery in databases? Explain.
2. Elaborate the DENCLUE algorithm in detail.
3. What is Distance Measure?
4. List out any Four Density Functions in Clustering.
5. How to solve the complexity in DBSCAN.
6. Write down the steps of Optics Algorithm?
7. How to implement the density based clustering algorithms in very Large Datasets.

CHAPTER IV

OUTLIER MINING

4.1.   Introduction

Outliers regarded as a noisy data in statistics has turned out to be an important problem which is being researched in diverse fields of research and application domains. Outlier detection aims to find patterns in data that do not confirm to the expected behavior. It is extensive used in a wide variety of applications such as military surveillance [Anscombe F.J and Guttman I, 1960] for enemy activities, intrusion detection in cyber security [Manikopoulos C and Papavassiliou S, 2002], fraud detection for credit cards [DorronSoro J.R et al., 1997], insurance or health care and fault detection in safety critical systems [Bronstein A et al., 2001].

The importance in data is due to the fact that can translate into actionable information in a wide variety of applications. An anomalous traffic pattern in a computer network could mean that a hacked computer is sending out sensitive data to an unauthorized destination [Kumar V, 2002]. An abnormal MRI image may indicate presence of malignant tumors [Spence C et al., 2001; Lin J et al., 2005]. Outliers in credit card transaction data can indicate credit card or identity theft [Aleskerov E, et al., 1997; Brause R et al., 1999]. Abnormal readings from a space craft sensor can signify a fault in some component of the space craft [Fujimaki R,et al., 2005].

Most of the previous studies on outlier detection were conducted in the field of statistics and these studies can be broadly classified into three categories. The first category is distribution based, where a standard distribution (e.g. Normal, Poisson, etc.) is used to fit the data best. Outliers are defined based on the probability distribution. Over one hundred tests of this category, called discordancy tests, have been developed for different scenarios.

A key drawback of this category of tests is that most of the distributions are used univariate and are some tests that are multivariate (e.g. multivariate normal outliers). But for many KDD applications, the underlying distribution is unknown. Fitting the data with standard distributions is very costly and may not produce satisfactory results. The second category of outlier is a notion of distance based outliers [Knorr K.M and Ng R.T, 1998]. Their notion generalizes many notions from the distribution based approaches and enjoys better computational complexity than the traditional approaches.

Recently, density based approach have been proposed. In this approach, a Local Outlier Factor (LOF) is computed for each point. The LOF of a point is based on the ratios of the local density of the area around the point and the local densities of its neighbors. The size of a neighborhood of a point is determined by the area containing a user supplied Minimum number of Points (MinPts).

4.2.   Outlier Classification

An important aspect of an outlier detection technique is the nature of the desired outlier. Outliers can be classified into following three categories. They are point outliers, contextual outliers and collective outliers [Song X et al., 2007].

4.2.1. Point Outliers

For an instance if an individual data can be considered as anomalous with respect to the rest of data then the instance is termed as a point outlier. This is the simplest type of outlier and is the focus of majority of research focuses on an outlier detection. For example, in Fig 4.1 points O_1 and O_2 as well as the points in region and hence are point outliers since they are different from normal data points as a real life example, consider credit card fraud detection with data set corresponding to an individual's credit card transactions assuming data definition by only one feature: amount spent. A transaction for which the amount spent is very high compared to the normal range of expenditure for that person will be a point outlier.

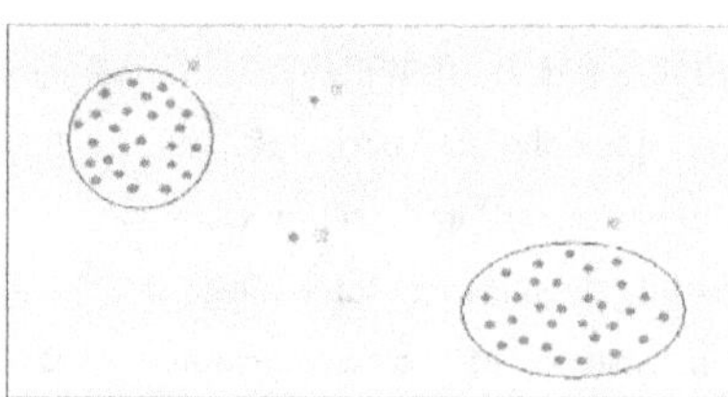

Fig. 4.1: Outliers in Dataset [Aggarwal C.C and Yu P.S, 2001]

4.2.2. Contextual Outliers

If a data instance is anomalous in a specific context (but not otherwise) then it is termed as a contextual outlier (also referred to as conditional outlier [Song X. et al., 2007]). The notion of a context is induced by the structure in the data set and has to be specified as a part of the problem formulation. Each data instance is defined using two sets of attributes:

- **Contextual attributes:** The contextual attributes are used to determine the context (or neighborhood) for that instance. For example, in spatial data sets, the longitude and latitude of a location are the contextual attributes. In time series data, time is a contextual attribute which determines the position of an instance on the entire sequence.

- **Behavioral attributes:** The behavioral attributes is defined as the non-contextual characteristics of an instance. For example, in a spatial data set describing the average rainfall of the entire world, the amount of rainfall at any location is a behavioral attribute.

The anomalous behavior is determined using the values for the behavioral attributes within a specific context. A data instance might be a contextual outlier in a given context but an identical data instance (in terms of behavioral attributes) could be considered normal in a different context. This property in key is identifying contextual and behavioral attributes for a contextual outlier detection technique [Song H et al., 2001]. The choice of applying a contextual outlier detection technique is determined by the meaningfulness of the contextual outliers in the target application domain.

Applying a contextual outlier detection technique makes sense if contextual attributes are readily available and therefore defining a context is straightforward. But it becomes difficult to apply such techniques and defining a context is not easy.

4.2.3. Collective Outliers

If a collection of related data instances are anomalous with respect to the entire data set, it is termed as a collective outlier [Desforges M et al., 1998]. The individual data instances in a collective outlier may not be outliers by themselves, but their occurrence together as a collection is anomalous. In Fig4.2 shows a human electrocardiogram output. The highlighted region denotes an outlier because the same low value exists for an abnormally long time (corresponding to an Adrenal Premature Contraction) [Arning A et al., 1996; Suzuki E et al., 2003]. It may be noted that low value by itself is not an outlier but its successive occurrence for long time is an outlier.

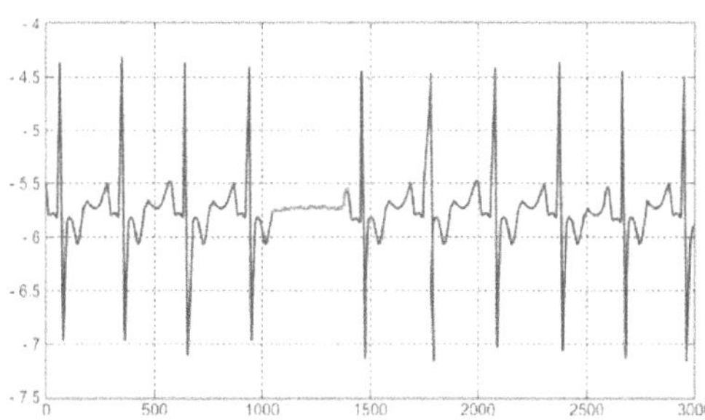

Fig. 4.2: Collective Outlier in a Human ECG Output Corresponding to an a Trial Premature Contraction [Forrest S et al., 1999]

as an example, consider a sequence of actions occurring in a computer as shown below:

.........http-web, buffer-overflow, http-web, http-web, smtp-mail, ftp, http-web, ssh, smtp-mail, http-web, ssh, buffer-overflow, ftp, http-web, ftp, smtp-mail, http-web......

The highlighted sequence of events [Ihler et al., 2006; Ide T and Kashima H, 2004] (buffer-overflow, ssh, ftp) correspond to a typical web based attack by a remote machine followed by copying of data from the host computer to remote destination via file transfer protocol. It should be noted that this collection of events is an outlier but the individual events are not outliers when they occur in other locations in the sequence. Collective outliers have been explored for sequence data [Forrest S et al., 1999; Sun P et al., 2006], graph data [Noble C. C et al., 2003] and spatial data.

[Sekar R et al., 2001]. It should be noted that while point outliers can occur in any data set, collective outliers can occur only in data sets in which data instances are related. In contrast, occurrence of contextual outliers depends on the availability of context attributes in the data. A point outlier or a collective outlier can also be a contextual outlier if analyzed with respect to a context. Thus a point outlier detection problem or collective outlier detection problem can be transformed to a contextual outlier detection problem by incorporating the context information [Dasgupta D and Nino F, 2000; Gwadera R et al., 2005].

4.3. Outlier Detection Methods

Outlier detection methods can be divided between univariate methods and multivariate methods that usually form most of the current body of research. Another fundamental taxonomy of outlier detection methods is between parametric (statistical) methods and nonparametric methods that are model free [Willams G.J et al., 2002]. Statistical parametric methods either assume a known underlying distribution of the observations [Hawkins D, 1980; Rousseeuw P and Leory A, 1987; Barnett V and Lewis T, 1994] or at least, they are based on statistical estimates of unknown distribution parameters [Hadi A.S, 1992; Abe N et al., 2006].

The methods flag as outliers those observations that deviate from the model assumptions. They are often unsuitable for high-dimensional data sets and for arbitrary data sets without prior knowledge of the underlying data distribution [Papadimitriou S et al., 2003]. Within the class of non parametric outlier detection methods one can set apart the data mining methods [Bakar Z et al., 2006] also called distance based methods. These methods are usually based on local distance measures and are capable of handling large databases [Knorr E et al., 2000; Jin W et al., 2001; Breunig M et al., 2000; Williams G.J et al., 2002; Bay S.D and Schwabacher M, 2003]. Another class of outlier detection methods is founded on clustering techniques where a cluster of small sizes can be considered as clustered outliers [Shekhar S et al., 2001; Shekhar S et al., 2002; Acuna E and Rodriguez C, 2004]. Vijayalakshmi M, Renuka Devi M [2012] whom proposed a method to identify both high and low density pattern clustering, further partition this class to hard classifiers and soft classifiers.

The former partition of data into two non-overlapping sets [Denning D.E, 1987] as outliers and non-outliers. The later offers a ranking by assigning each datum an outlier classification factor reflecting its degree of outlying-ness. Another related class of methods consists of detection techniques for spatial outliers [Agyemang M et al., 2006; Hofmeyr S.A et al., 1998]. These methods search for extreme observations or local instabilities with respect to neighbouring values, although these observations may not be significantly different from the entire population [Shekhar S and Lu C.T, 2001; Shekhar S and Lu C.T, 2002; Lu C et al., 2003].

4.3.1. *Univariate Outlier Detection Methods*

Most of the earliest univariate methods for outlier detection rely on the assumption of an underlying known distribution of the data which is assumed to be identically and independently distributed. Moreover, many discordance tests for detecting univariate outliers further assume that the distribution parameters and the type of expected outliers are also known [Barnett V and Lewis T, 1994].

A central assumption in statistical based methods for outlier detection is a generating model that allows a small number of observations to be randomly sampled from distributions $G_1,...G_k$, differing from the target distribution which is often taken to be a normal distribution. The outlier identification problem is then translated to the problem of identifying those observations that lie in a so called outlier region.

For any confidence coefficient α, $0 < \alpha < 1$, the α-outlier, region of the N (μ, σ^2) distribution is defined by

$$out\ (\alpha, \mu, \sigma^2) = \{x : \ |x - u| \ > z_q - \alpha / 2\ \sigma$$

where z_q is the q quintile of the N (0,1). A number x is α outlier with respect to F if x

ϵ out (α, μ, σ^2). Although traditionally the normal distribution has been used as the target distribution, this definition can be easily extended to any uni-modal symmetric distribution with positive density function including the multivariate case. The outlier definition does not identify which of the observations are contaminated, i.e., resulting from distributions $G_1,.., G_k$ but rather it indicates those observations that lie in the outlier region.

4.3.1.1. Single Step Vs. Sequential Procedures

Single step procedures identify all outliers at once as opposed to successive elimination or addition of datum. In the sequential procedures at each step one observation is tested for being an outlier. With respect to equation a common rule for finding the outlier region in a single step identifier is given by

$$\text{out}\,(\,\alpha_n,\ \hat{\mu}_n\,,\hat{\sigma}_n{}^2\,) = \{\,x : |\,x - \hat{\mu}_n\,| > g\,(\,n,\ \alpha_n\,)\hat{\sigma}_n\}$$

where n is the size of the sample; $\hat{\mu}_n$ and $\hat{\sigma}_n$ are the estimated mean and standard deviation of the target distribution based on the sample, α_n denotes the confidence coefficient following the correction for multiple comparison tests and g (n, α_n) defines the limits (critical number of standard deviations) of the outlier regions.

Traditionally, $\hat{\mu}_n$, $\hat{\sigma}_n$ are the estimated respectively by the sample mean, $\bar{x}_n$ and the sample standard deviation, S_n. Since these estimates are highly affected by the presence of outliers, many procedures often replace them by other more robust. The multiple comparisons correction is used when several statistical tests are being performed simultaneously. While a given α value may be appropriate to decide whether a single observation lies in the outlier region (i.e., a single comparison) this is not the case for a set of several comparisons. In order to avoid spurious positives the α-value needs to be lowered to account for the number of performed comparisons.

The simplest and most conservative approach is the Bonferroni's correction, which sets the value for the entire set of *n* comparisons equal to α, by taking α value for each comparison equal to α/n. Another popular and simple correction uses $\alpha_n = 1-(1-\alpha)^{1/n}$. The traditional Bonferroni's method is "quasi-optimal" when the observations are independent which is in most cases unrealistic. The critical value g (n, α_n) is often specified by numerical procedures such as Monte Carlo simulations for different sample sizes.

4.3.1.2. Inward and Outward Procedures

Sequential identifiers can be classified into inward and outward procedures. In inward testing or forward selection methods at each step of the procedure the "most extreme observation", i.e., the one with the largest outlying-ness measure is tested for being an outlier [Hadi A.S, 1992]. If it is declared as an outlier, it is deleted from the dataset and the procedure is repeated. If it is declared as a non-outlying observation the procedure terminates.

In outward testing procedures the sample of observations is first reduced to a smaller sample (e.g., by a factor of two) while the removed observations are kept in a reservoir. The statistics are calculated on the basis of the reduced sample and then the removed observations in the reservoir are tested in reverse order to indicate whether they are outliers. If an observation is declared as a non outlying observation it is.

4.3.2. Multivariate Outlier Detection Methods

In many cases multivariable observations cannot be detected as outliers when each variable is considered independently. Outlier detection is possible only when multivariate analysis is performed and the interactions among different variables are compared within the class of data. A simple example can be seen in Fig 4.3 which presents data points having two measures on a two dimensional space. The lower left observation is clearly a multivariate outlier but not a univariate one.

When considering each measure separately with respect to the spread of values along the x and y axes, fall close to the center of the univariate distributions. Thus, the test for outliers must take into account the relationships between the two variables, which in this case appear abnormal.

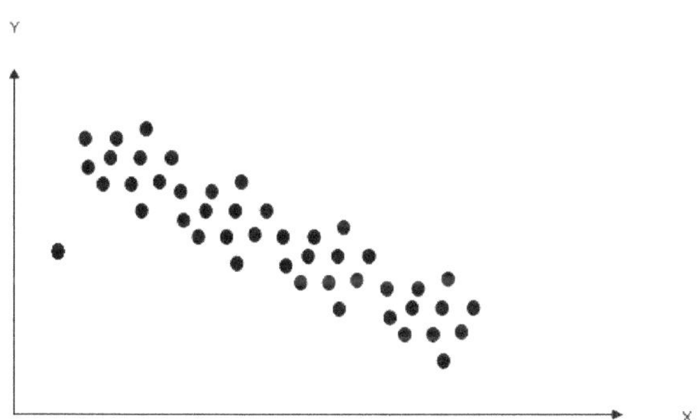

Fig. 4.3: A Two Dimensional Space with One Outlying Observation (Lower left corner) [Acuna E and Rodriguez C, 2004]

Data sets with multiple outliers or clusters of outliers are subject to masking and swamping effects. Although not mathematically rigorous, the following definitions from [Acuna E and Rodriguez C, 2004] give an intuitive understanding for these effects.

Masking effect: It is said that one outlier masks a second outlier, if the second outlier can be considered as an outlier only by itself but not in the presence of the first outlier. Thus, after the deletion of the first outlier the second instance is emerged as an outlier. Masking occurs when a cluster of outlying observations skewed the mean and the covariance estimates toward it and the resulting distance of the outlying point from the mean is small.

Swamping effect: It is said that one outlier swamps a second observation, if the later can be considered as an outlier only under the presence of the first one. In other words, after the deletion of the first outlier the second observation becomes a non-outlying observation. Swamping occurs when a group of outlying instances skews the mean and the covariance estimates toward it and away from other non-outlying instances and the resulting distance from these instances to the mean is large making them look like outliers.

4.3.2.1. Statistical Methods for Multivariate Outlier Detection

Multivariate outlier detection procedures can be divided to statistical methods that are based on estimated distribution parameters and data mining related methods that are typically parameter free. Statistical methods for multivariate outlier detection often indicate those observations that are located relatively far from the center of the data distribution. Such a definition is based on a single, global criterion determined by the parameters r and β.

The time complexity of the algorithm is $O(p_n^2)$ where p is the number of features and n is the sample size. Hence, it is not an adequate definition to use with very large datasets. Moreover, this definition can lead to problems when the data set has both dense and sparse regions. Alternatively, Ramaswamy S et al., [2000] suggest the following definition: given two integers v and l (v, l), outliers are defined to be the top l sorted observations having the largest distance to their v^{th} nearest neighbor. One shortcoming of this definition is that it only considers the distance to the vth neighbor and ignores information about closer observations.

An alternative is to define outliers as those observations having a large average distance to the v-th nearest neighbors. The drawback of this alternative is that it takes longer to be calculated.

Clustering based methods consider a cluster of small sizes including the size of one observation, as clustered outliers. Some examples for such methods are the Partitioning Around Medoids (PAM) and the Clustering Large Applications (CLARA) a modified version of the latter for spatial outliers called CLARANS and a dimension based method [Barbara D and Chen P, 2000]. Clustering methods are not always optimized for outlier detection. In most cases, the outlier detection criteria are implicit and cannot easily be inferred from the clustering procedures.

Spatial methods are closely related to clustering methods. Lu C et al., [2003] define a spatial outlier as a spatially referenced object whose non-spatial attribute values are significantly different from the values of its neighborhood. The authors indicate that the methods of spatial statistics can be generally classified into two sub-categories: quantitative method and graphic method. Quantitative method provides tests to distinguish spatial outliers from the remainder of data. Two representative approaches in this category are the Scatter plot and the Moran scatter plot.

Graphic method is based on visualization of spatial data which high lights spatial outliers. Variogram clouds and pocket plots are two examples for these methods suggest using a Multi Dimensional Scaling (MDS) that represents the similarities between objects spatially as in a map. MDS seeks to find the best configuration of the observations in a low dimensional space. Both metric and non metric forms of MDS are proposed [Penny K.I and Jolliffe I.T, 2001; Chen D et al., 2005]. As indicated above Ng R.T and Han J [1994] developed a clustering method for spatial data mining called CLARANS which is based on randomized search.

The authors suggest two spatial data mining algorithms that use CLARANS. Shekhar S et al., [2001] introduced a method for detecting spatial outliers in graph data set. The method is based on the distribution property of the difference between an attribute value and the average attribute value of its neighbors. Shekhar S et al., [2002] proposed a unified approach to evaluate spatial outlier detection methods. Lu C et al., [2003] proposed a suite of spatial outlier detection algorithms to minimize false detection of spatial outliers when their neighborhood contains true spatial outliers. Applications of spatial outliers [Murray A.T and Estivvil Castro V, 1998] can be found in fields where spatial information plays an important role, such as, ecology, geographic information systems, transportation, climatology, location based services, public health and public[Laurikkala J et al., 2000].

Accordingly, those observations with a large Mahalanobis distance are indicated as outliers. Masking and swamping effects play an important role in the adequacy of the Mahalanobis distance as a criterion for outlier detection. Namely, masking effects might decrease the Mahalanobis distance of an outlier [Brockett P et al., 1998]. This might happen for example, when a small cluster of outliers attracts $\bar{x}_n$ and inflate v_n towards its direction. On the other hand, swamping effects might increase the Mahalanobis distance of non-outlying observations. For example, when a small cluster of outliers attracts $\bar{x}_n$ and inflate v_n away from the pattern of the majority of the observations [Penny K.I and Jolliffe, 2001].

4.3.2.2. Multivariate Robust Measures

The distribution mean (measuring the location) and the variance covariance (measuring the shape) are the two most commonly used statistics for data analysis in the presence of outliers in one dimensional procedure. The robust estimates of the multidimensional distribution parameters can often improve the performance of the detection procedures in the presence of outliers. Hadi A.S [1992] addressed the outlier problem and proposed to replace the mean vector by a vector of variable medians and to compute the covariance matrix for the subset of those observations with the smallest Mahalanobis distance [Penny KI and Jolliffe I.T, 2001].

Steinwart I et al., [2005] propose a robust estimate for the covariance matrix, which is based on weighted observations according to their distance from the center. The authors also propose a method for a low dimensional projection of the dataset. The Generalized Principle Component Analysis (GPCA) reveals those dimensions which display outliers. Other robust estimators of the location (centroid) and the shape (covariance matrix) include the Minimum Covariance Determinant (MCD) and the minimum volume ellipsoid.

4.3.3. *Statistical Methods*

Statistical outlier detection methods [Manikopoulos C and Papavassiliou S, 2002] rely on the statistical approaches that assume a distribution or probability model to fit the given dataset. The outliers are those points that do not agree with or conform to the underlying model of the data in the dataset distribution. The statistical outlier detection methods can be broadly classified into two categories, i.e., the parametric method and the non-parametric method. The major differences between these two classes of methods lie in that the parametric method assume the underlying distribution of the given data and estimate the parameters of the distribution model from the given data while the non-parametric method do not assume any knowledge of distribution characteristics[Roberts S, 1999].

Statistical outlier detection methods (parametric and non-parametric) typically take two stages for detecting outliers, i.e., the training stage and test stage [Para L et al., 1996].

- **Training stage:** The training stage mainly involves fitting a statistical model or building data profiles based on the given data. Statistical techniques can be performed in a supervised, semi supervised and unsupervised manner. Supervised techniques estimate the probability density for normal instances and outliers. Semi supervised techniques estimate the probability density for either normal instances or outliers, depending on the availability of labels. Unsupervised techniques determine a statistical model or profile which fits all the majority of the instances in the given data set.

- **Test stage:** The next step of the probabilistic model or profile is to determine if a given data instance is an outlier with respect to the model/profile or not. This involves computing the posterior probability of the test instance to be generated by the constructed model or the deviation from the constructed data profile. For example, find the distance of the data instance from the estimated mean and declare any point above a threshold to be an outlier.

4.3.3.1. Parametric Method

Parametric statistical outlier detection methods [Chow C and Yeung D.Y, 2002] explicitly assume the probabilistic or distribution model(s) for the given data set. Model parameters can be estimated using the training data based on the distribution assumption. The major parametric outlier detection methods are Gaussian model and Regression model.

Gaussian Models

Detecting outliers based on Gaussian distribution models have been intensively studied. The training stage typically performs estimation of the mean and variance (or standard deviation) of the Gaussian distribution using Maximum Likelihood Estimates (MLE). To ensure that the distribution assumed by human users is the optimal or close-to-optima underlying distribution the data fit, statistical discord any tests are normally conducted in the test stage [Angiulli F and Pizzuti C, 2005].

The rationale is that some small portions of points that have small probability of occurrence in the population are identified as outliers. The commonly used outlier tests for normal distributions are the mean variance test and box plot test.

In the mean variance test for a Gaussian distribution $N(\mu, \sigma^2)$, where the population has a mean μ and variance σ, outliers can be considered to be points that lie three or more standard deviations (i.e., $\geq 3\sigma$) away from the mean. This test is general and can be applied to some other commonly used distributions such as student the distribution and Poisson distribution which feature a fatter tail and a longer right tail than a normal distribution, respectively.

The box plot test draws on the box plot to graphically depict the distribution of data using five major attributes, i.e., smallest non-outlier observation (min), lower quartile (Q_1), median, upper quartile (Q_3) and largest non-outlier observation (max). The quantity Q_3-Q_1 is called the Inter Quartile Range (IQR). IQR provides a means to indicate the boundary beyond which the data will be labeled as outliers, a data instance will be labeled as an outlier if it is located 1.5*IQR times lower than Q_1 or 1.5*IQR times higher than Q_3.

A mixture of probabilistic models may be used if a single model is not sufficient for the purpose of data modeling. If labeled data are available, two separate models can be constructed, one for the normal data and another for the outliers. The membership probability of the new instances can be quantified and they are labeled as outliers if their membership probability of outlier probability model is higher than that of the model of the normal data. The mixture of probabilistic models [Solberg H.E and Lahti, 2005] can also be applied to unlabeled data, that is, the whole training data are modeled using a mixture of models. A test instance is considered to be an outlier if it is found that it does not belong to any of the constructed models.

Regression Models

If the probabilistic model is unknown regression can be employed for model construction. The regression analysis aims to find a dependence of one/more random variable(s) y on another one/more variable(s) x. This involves examining the conditional probability distribution y|x. Outlier detection using regression techniques are intensively applied to time series data [Li X, 2007]. The training stage involves constructing a regression model that fits the data. The regression model can either be a linear or non linear model depending on the choice from users. The test stage tests the regression model by evaluating each data instance against the model. More specifically, such test involves comparing the actual instance value and its projected value produced by the regression model. A data point is labeled as an outlier if a remarkable deviation occurs between the actual value and its expected value produced by the regression model.

The two ways of the data in the dataset to build the regression model for outlier detection namely the reverse search and direct search methods. The reverse search method constructs the regression model by using all data available and then the data with the greatest error are considered as outliers and excluded from the model. The direct search approach constructs a model based on a portion of data and then adds new data points incrementally when the preliminary model construction has been finished. Then, the model is extended by adding the most fitting data, which are those objects in the rest of the population that have the least deviations from the model constructed thus far. The data added to the model in the last round, considered to be the least fitting data are regarded to be outliers.

4.3.3.2. Non-Parametric Method

The outlier detection techniques in this category do not make any assumptions about the statistical distribution of the data. The most popular approaches for outlier detection in this category are histograms and Kernel density function methods.

Histograms

The most popular non-parametric statistical technique is to use histograms to maintain a profile of data. Histogram techniques by nature are based on the frequency or counting of data. The histogram based outlier detection approach is typically applied when the data has a single feature. Mathematically, a histogram for a feature of data consists of a number of disjoint bins (or buckets) and the data are mapped into one (and only one) bin. Represented graphically by the histogram graph the height of bins corresponds to the number of observations that fall into the bins. Thus, let n be the total number of instances, k be the total number of bins and m_i be the number of data point in the ith bin ($1 \leq i \leq k$), the histogram satisfies the following condition n = P_k.

$$n = \sum_{i=1}^{k} m_i$$

The training stage involves building histograms based on the different values taken by that feature in the training data. The histogram techniques typically define a measure between a new test instance and the histogram based profile to determine if it is an outlier or not. The measure is defined based on how the histogram is constructed in the first place. Specifically, there are three possible ways for building a histogram.

- The histogram can be constructed only based on normal data. In this case, the histogram only represents the profile for normal data. The test stage evaluates whether the feature value in the test instance falls in any of the populated bins of the constructed histogram. If not the test instance is labeled as an outlier.

- The histogram can be constructed only based on outliers. As such, the histogram captures the profile for outliers. A test instance that falls into one of the populated bins is labeled as an outlier. Such techniques are particularly popular in intrusion detection community [Roberts S, 1999] and fraud detection.

- The histogram can be constructed based on a mixture of normal data and outliers. This is the typical case where histogram is constructed. Since normal data typically dominate the whole data set, thus the histogram represents an approximated profile of normal data. The sparsely of a bin in the histogram can be defined as the ratio of frequency of this bin against the average frequency of all the bins in the histogram. A bin is considered as sparse if such ratio is lower than a user specified threshold. All the data instance falling into the sparse bins are labeled as outliers.

The first and second ways for constructing histogram, rely on the availability of labeled instances while the third one does not. For multivariate data, a common approach is to construct feature wise histograms. In the test stage, the probability for each feature value of the test data is calculated and then aggregated to generate so called outlier score. A low probability value corresponds a higher outlier score of that test instance.

The aggregation of per feature likelihoods for calculating outlier score is typically done using the following equation:

$$\text{outlier\_score} = \sum_{f \varepsilon F} w_f (1\text{-}p_f) \, / \, |F|$$

where w_f denotes the weight assigned for feature f, p_f denotes the probability for the value of feature f and F denotes the set of features of the dataset. Such histogram based aggregation techniques have been used in intrusion detection in system call data, fraud detection, damage detection in structures, network intrusion detection, web based attack detection, Packet Header Anomaly Detection (PHAD), Application Layer Anomaly Detection (ALAD). Also, a substantial amount of research has been done in the field of outlier detection for sequential data (primarily to detect intrusions in computer system call data) using histogram based techniques. These techniques are fundamentally similar to the instance based histogram approaches as described above but are applied to sequential data to detect collective outliers.

Histogram based detection methods are simple to implement and are quite popular in domain such as intrusion detection, fraud detection and damage detection in structures. But one key shortcoming of such techniques for multivariate data is that they are not able to capture the interactions between different attributes. An outlier might have attribute values that are individually very frequent, but their combination is very rare. This shortcoming will become more salient when dimensionality of data is high. A feature-wise histogram technique will not be able to detect such kinds of outliers. Another challenge for such techniques is that users need to determine an optimal size of the bins to construct the histogram.

Kernel Functions

A popular non-parametric approach for outlier detection is the parzen windows estimation. This involves using kernel functions to approximate the actual density distribution. A new instance which lies in the low probability area of this density is declared to be an outlier.

Formally, if $x_1, x_2 \ldots x_n$ are IID (Independently and Identically Distributed) samples of a random variable x, then the kernel density approximation of its Probability Density Function (pdf) is

$$F_h(x) = 1 \, / \, N_h \sum_{i=1}^{n} K(x\text{-}x_i) \, / \, h$$

where K is kernel function and h is the bandwidth (smoothing parameter). Quite often, K is taken to be a standard Gaussian function with mean $\mu = 0$ and variance $\sigma^2 = 1$.

Novelty detection using kernel function is presented for detecting novelties in oil flow data [Bishop C, 1994]. A test instance is declared to be novel if it belongs to the low density area of the learnt density function. Similar application of parzen windows is proposed for network intrusion detection and for mammographic image analysis. A semi-supervised probabilistic approach is proposed to detect novelties. Kernel functions are used to estimate the Probability Distribution Function (pdf) for the normal instances. Recently, kernel functions are used in outlier detection in sensor networks. Kernel density estimation of pdf is applicable to both univariate and multivariate data. However, the pdf estimation for multivariate data is much more computationally expensive than the univariate data.

Statistical outlier detection method feature some advantages [Petrovskiy M.I, 2003]. The methods are very efficient and it is possible to reveal the meaning of the outliers found. In addition, often the model constructed and presented in a compact form, makes it possible to detect outliers without storing the original datasets that are usually of large sizes. However, the statistical outlier detection methods, particularly the parametric methods, suffer from some key drawbacks. First, they are typically not applied in a multi dimensional scenario because the most distribution models typically apply to the univariate feature space. Thus, the unsuitable even for moderate multidimensional data sets [Manikopolos C and Papavassilio S, 2002]. This greatly limits their applicability as in most practical applications the data is multiple or even high dimensional.

In addition, a lack of the prior knowledge regarding the underlying distribution of the dataset makes the distribution based methods difficult to use in practical applications. A single distribution may not model the entire data because the data may originate from multiple distributions. Finally, the quality of results cannot be guaranteed because they are largely dependent on the distribution chosen to fit the data. It is not guaranteed that the data being examined fit the assumed distribution if there is no estimate of the distribution density based on the empirical data.

Constructing such tests for hypothesis verification in complex combinations of distributions is a non-trivial task whatsoever. Even if the model is properly chosen, finding the values of parameters requires complex procedures. From above discussion, the statistical methods are rather limited to large real world databases which typically have many different fields and it is not easy to characterize the multivariate distribution of exemplars. For non-parametric statistical methods, such as histogram and kernel function methods, they do not have the problem of distribution assumption that the parametric methods suffer and they both can deal with data streams containing continuously arriving data. However, they are not appropriate for handling high dimensional data[Forrest S et al., 2004]. Histogram methods are effective for a single feature analysis but they lose much of their effectiveness for multi or high dimensional data because they lack the ability to analyze multiple features simultaneously. This prevents them from detecting subspace outliers. Kernel function methods are appropriate only for relatively low dimensional data as well. When the dimensionality of data is high, the density estimation using kernel functions becomes rather computationally expensive, making it inappropriate for handling high dimensional data streams.

Distribution based approaches develop statistical models (typically for the normal behavior) from the given data and then apply a statistical test to determine if an object belongs to this model or not [Hawkins D, 1980; Barnett V and Lewis T, 1994]. Objects that have low probability to belong to the statistical model are declared as outliers. However, Distribution based approaches cannot be applied in multi dimensional scenarios because they are univariate in nature. In addition, a prior knowledge of the data distribution is required, making the distribution based approaches difficult to be used in practical applications [Hawkins D, 1980].

4.3.4. *Distance Based Methods*

There are number of different ways for defining outliers from the perspective of distance related metrics. Most existing metrics used for distance based outlier detection techniques are defined based upon the concepts of local neighborhood or k-Nearest Neighbors (k-NN) of the data points. The notion of distance based outliers does not assume any underlying data distributions and generalizes many concepts from distribution based methods. Moreover, distance based methods scale better to multi dimensional space and can be computed much more efficiently than the statistical based methods.

In distance based methods, distance between data points is needed to be computed. Use any of the L_p metrics like the Manhattan distance or Euclidean distance metrics for measuring the distance between a pair of points. Alternately, for some other application domains with presence of categorical data (e.g., text documents), non-metric distance functions can also be used, making the distance-based definition of outliers very general. Data normalization is normally carried out in order to normalize the different scales of data features before outlier detection is performed.

The basic distance based approach is that implemented in the DB (p,d) method. The DB (p, d) method is based on the following definition of an outlier. An object o is an outlier if at least the pth fraction of all objects of the database are at a distance greater than d from the given object o. Various algorithms for this method have been suggested, which are designed for different models of data storage and datasets of different dimensions.

The index based algorithm, for each object, calculates the number of objects belonging to the d-neighborhood of the object (i.e., objects located at a distance not exceeding d). To find the neighbors, a priori constructed index is used. The complexity of the algorithm is quadratic.

The nested loop algorithm is based on partitioning the entire set of objects into blocks, such that, on each step, distances between objects belonging to two blocks only are calculated. This algorithm also has quadratic complexity; however, it does not require preliminary construction of the index, which is a time consuming operation.

In the cell based algorithm, the complexity of examining all pairs of objects is reduced through a preliminary partition of the space into cells and construction of estimates for distances between the objects.

4.3.4.1. Local Neighborhood Method

The first notion of distance based outliers, called DB (k, λ) outlier, is due to Knorr K.M [1998] and defined as follows. A point p in a data set is a DB(k, λ) outlier, with respect to the parameters k and λ, if no more than k points in the data set are at a distance λ or less (i.e., λ neighborhood) from p. This definition of outliers is intuitively simple and straightforward. The major disadvantage of this method, however, its sensitivity to the parameter λ that is difficult to specify a priori. As known, when the data dimensionality increases, it becomes increasingly difficult to specify an appropriate circular local neighborhood (delimited by λ) for outlier-ness evaluation of each point since most of the points are likely to lie in a thin shell about any point. Thus, a too small λ will cause the algorithm to detect all points as outliers, whereas no point will be detected as outliers if a too large λ is picked up. In other words, one needs to choose an appropriate λ with a very high degree of accuracy in order to find a modest number of points that can then be defined as outliers [Duan L et al., 2007].

To facilitate the choice of parameter values, this first local neighborhood distance based outlier definition extended and so called as DB (pct, dmin). Outlier is proposed which defines an object in a dataset as a DB (pct, d_{min}) outlier if at least pct% of the objects in the datasets has the distance larger than d_{min} from this object [Knorr K. M, 1998]. Similar to DB (k, λ) outlier, this method essentially delimits the local neighborhood of data points using the parameter d_{min} and measures the outlier-ness of a data point based on the percentage, instead of the absolute number of data points falling into this specified local neighborhood. As pointed out by Knorr K. M [1998], DB (pct, d_{min}) is quite general and is able to unify the existing statistical detection methods using discordancy tests for outlier detection. For example, DB (pct, d_{min}) unifies the definition of outliers using a normal distribution based discordancy test with pct = 0.9988 and d_{min} = 0.13. The specification of pct is obviously more intuitive and easier than the specification of k in DB (k, λ) outliers [Knorr K. M, 1998]. However, DB (pct, d_{min}) outlier suffers a similar problem as DB (pct, d_{min}) outlier in specifying the local neighborhood parameter d_{min}.

To efficiently calculate the number (or percentage) of data points falling into the local neighborhood of each point, three classes of algorithms as nested loop, index based and cell based algorithms. For easy of presentation, these three algorithms are discussed for detecting DB (k, λ) outlier. The nested loop algorithm uses two nested loops to compute DB (k, λ) outlier. The outer loop considers each point in the dataset while the inner loop computes for each point in the outer loop the number (or percentage) of points in the dataset falling into the specified λ neighborhood.

This algorithm has the advantage that it does not require the indexing structure be constructed at all that may be rather expensive at most of the time, though it has a quadratic complexity with respect to the number of points in the dataset. The index based algorithm involves calculating the number of points belonging to the λ neighborhood of each data by intensively using a pre constructed multi dimensional index structure such as R* tree to facilitate k-NN search. The complexity of the algorithm is approximately logarithmic with respect to the number of the data points in the dataset.

However, the construction of index structures is sometimes very expensive and the quality of the index structure constructed is not easy to guarantee. In the cell based algorithm, the data space is partitioned into cells and all the data points are mapped into cells. By means of the cell size that is known a priori, estimates of pair wise distance of data points are developed, whereby heuristics (pruning properties) are presented to achieve fast outlier detection. It is shown that three passes over the dataset are sufficient for constructing the desired partition. More precisely, the 'd' dimensional space is partitioned into cells with side length of $\lambda_2\sqrt{d}$.

Thus, the distance between points in any two neighboring cells is guaranteed to be at most λ. As a result, if for a cell the total number of points in the cell and its neighbors is greater than k, then none of the points in the cell can be outliers. This property is used to eliminate the vast majority of points that cannot be outliers. The points belonging to cells that are more than three cells apart are more than a distance λ apart. As a result, if the number of points contained in all cells that are at most three cells away from the given cell is less than k, then all points in the cell are definitely outliers.

Finally, for those points that belong to a cell that cannot be categorized as either containing only outliers or only non-outliers, only points from neighboring cells that are at most three cells away need to be considered in order to determine whether or not they are outliers. Based on the above properties, Knorr K. M [1998] proposed a three pass algorithm for computing outliers in large databases. The time complexity of this cell based algorithm is O (cd + N), where c is a number that is inversely proportional to λ.

This complexity is linear with dataset size N but exponential with the number of dimensions d. As a result, due to the exponential growth in the number of cells as the number of dimensions is increased, the cell based algorithm starts to perform poorly than the nested loop for datasets with dimensions of four or higher. The similar definition of outlier is proposed to calculate the number of points falling into the w radius of each data point. These points as outliers that have low neighborhood density [Eskin E, et al., 2002].

Consider this definition of outliers as the same as that for DB (k, λ) outlier, differing only that this method does not present the threshold k explicitly in the definition. As the computation of the local density for each point is expensive, Eskin E et al., [2002] proposed a clustering method for an efficient estimation.

The basic idea of such approximation is to use the size of a cluster to approximate the local density of all the data in this cluster. It uses the fixed width clustering for density estimation due to its good efficiency in dealing with large data sets.

4.3.4.2. k-NN Distance Method

There have also been a few distance based outlier detection [Byers S.D and Raftery A.E, 1998] methods utilizing the k nearest neighbors (k-NN) in measuring the outlier-ness of data points in the dataset. The first proposal uses the distance to the kth nearest neighbors of every point, denoted as D^k, to rank points so that outliers can be more efficiently discovered and ranked [Ramaswamy S, et al., 2000]. Based on the notion of D^k, the following definition for D^k_n outlier is given: Given k and n, a point is an outlier if the distance to its kth nearest neighbor of the point is smaller than the corresponding value for no more than n – 1 other point. Essentially, this definition of outliers considers the top n objects having the highest D^k values in the dataset as outliers.

The three different algorithms similar to the computation of DB(k,λ) i.e., the nested loop algorithm, the index based algorithm and the partition based algorithms are proposed to compute D^k for each data point efficiently [Sun J et al., 2009]. The nested loop algorithm for computing outliers simply computes, for each input point p, D^k the distance of between p and its kth nearest neighbor. It then sorts the data and selects the top n points with the maximum D^k values. In order to compute D^k for points, the algorithm scans the database for each point p.

For a point p, a list of its k nearest points is maintained and for each point q from the database which is considered, a check is made to see if the distance between p and q is smaller than the distance of the kth nearest neighbor found so far. If so, q is included in the list of the k nearest neighbors for p. The moment that the list contains more than k neighbors, then the point that is far away from p is deleted from the list. In this algorithm, since only one point is processed at a time, the database would need to be scanned n times, where n is the number of points in the database. The computational complexity is in the order of $O(n^2)$, which is rather expensive for large datasets.

The index based algorithm draws on index structure such as R*tree to speed up the computation. If all the points stored in a spatial index like R*tree, the following pruning optimization can be applied to reduce the number of distance computations. Suppose that have computed for point p by processing a portion of the input points. The value that has is clearly an upper bound for the actual D^k of p. If the minimum distance between p and the Minimum Bounding Rectangles (MBR) of a node in the R*tree exceeds the value that have anytime in the algorithm, then claim that none of the points in the sub tree rooted under the node will be among the k nearest neighbors of p. This optimization enables us to prune entire sub trees that do not contain relevant points to the k-NN for p [Du W et al., 2006].

The major idea underlying the partition based algorithm is to first partition the data space and then prune partitions as soon as it can be determines that they cannot contain outliers. Partition based algorithm is subject to the pre-processing step in which data space is split into cells and data partitions, together with the Minimum Bounding Rectangles (MBR) of data partitions are generated. Since n will typically be very small, this additional pre-processing step performed at the granularity of partitions rather than points is worthwhile as it can eliminate a significant number of points as outlier candidates. This partition based algorithm takes the following four steps [Knorr E et al., 2000]:

- First, a clustering algorithm is used to cluster the data and each cluster as a separate partition.
- For each partition P, the lower and upper bounds (denoted as P.lower and P.upper, respectively) on D^k for points in the partition are computed. For every point $p \in P$, have P.lower $\leq D^k(p) \leq$ P.upper.

- The candidate partitions, the partitions containing points which are candidates for outliers, are identified. Suppose minD^{k}Dist could be computed, the lower bound on D^k for the n outliers. Then, if P.upper < minD^{k}Dist, none of the points in P can possibly be outliers and are safely pruned. Thus, only partitions P for which P.upper ≥ minD^{k}Dist are chosen as candidate partitions.

- Finally, the outliers are computed from among the points in the candidate partitions obtained in third Step. For each candidate partition P. P.neighbors denote the neighboring partitions of P, which are all the partitions within distance P.upper from P. Points belonging to neighboring partitions of P are the only points that need to be examined when computing D^k for each point in P.

The D^k_n outlier is further extended by considering for each point the sum of its k nearest neighbors. This extension is motivated by the fact that the definition of D^k merely considers the distance between an object with its kth nearest neighbor, entirely ignoring the distances between this object and it's another k−1 nearest neighbors. This drawback may make D^k fail to give an accurate measurement of outlier-ness of data points in some cases. This method is also used for anomaly detection. The idea of k-NN based distance metric can be extended to consider the k nearest dense regions. The recent methods are the largest cluster method and grid Outlying Detection Factor (ODF) as discussed below.

A distance based method for labeling wireless network traffic records in the data stream used as either normal or intrusive. Let d be the largest distance of an instance to the centroid of the largest cluster.

Any instance or cluster that has a distance greater than αd (α ≥ 1) to the largest cluster is defined as an attack. This method is referred to as the largest cluster method. It can also be used to detect outliers.

It takes the following several steps for outlier detection [Barbara D et al., 2001]:

- Find the largest cluster, i.e. the cluster with largest number of instances and label it as normal. Let c_0 be the centroid of this cluster.

- Sort the remaining clusters in ascending order based on the distance from their cluster centroid to c_0.

- Label all the instances that have a distance to c0 greater than αd, where α is a human-specified parameter.

- Label all the other instances as normal.

When used in dealing with projected anomalies detection for high dimensional data streams, this method suffers from the following limitations:

- First and most importantly, this method does not take into account the nature of outliers in high dimensional data sets and is unable to explore subspaces to detect projected outliers.

- K-means clustering is used in this method as the backbone enabling technique for detecting intrusions. This poses difficulty for this method to deal with data streams. K-means clustering requires iterative optimization of clustering centroids to gradually achieve better clustering results. This optimization process involves multiple data scans, which is infeasible in the context of data streams.

- A strong assumption is made in this method that all the normal data will appear in a single cluster (i.e., the largest cluster), which is not properly substantiated. This assumption may be too rigid in some applications. It is possible that the normal data are distributed in two or more clusters that correspond to a few varying normal behaviors. For a simple instance, the network traffic volume is usually high during the daytime and becomes low late in the night. Thus, network traffic volume may display several clusters to represent behaviors exhibiting at different time of the day. In such case, the largest cluster is apparently not where all the normal cases are only residing.

- In this method, one needs to specify the parameter α. The method is rather sensitive to this parameter whose best value is not obvious what so ever. First, the distance scale between data will be rather different in various subspaces; the distance between any pair of data is naturally increased when it is evaluated in a subspace with higher dimension, compared to in a lower dimensional subspace. Therefore, specifying an ad-hoc α value for each subspace evaluated is rather tedious and difficult. Second, α is also heavily affected by the number of clusters the clustering method produces, i.e., k. intuitively, when the number of clusters k is small, D will become relatively large, then α should be set relatively small accordingly and vice versa.

Recently, an extension of the notion of k-NN, called Grid-ODF, from the k nearest objects to the k nearest dense regions is developed [Aleskerov E et al., 1997]. This method employed the sum of the distances between each data point and its k nearest dense regions to rank data points. This enables the algorithm to measure the outlier-ness of data points from a more global perspective. Grid ODF takes into account the mechanisms used in detecting both global and local outliers [Gao Y. Xia, 2006]. In the local perspective, human examine the point's immediate neighborhood and consider it as an outlier if its neighborhood density is low.

The global observation considers the dense regions where the data points are densely populated in the data space. Specifically, the neighboring density of the point serves as a good indicator of its outlying degree from the local perspective. A new measurement of outlying factor of data points, called Outlying Degree Factor (ODF), is proposed to measure the outlier-ness of points from both the global and local perspectives. The ODF of a point p is defined as follows:

$$ODF(P) = K\_DF(p) / NDF(p)$$

where K_DF (p) denotes the average distance between p and its k nearest dense cells and NDF (p) denotes number of points falling into the cell to which p belongs. In order to implement the computation of ODF of points efficiently, grid structure is used to partition the data space. The main idea of grid based data space partition is to super impose a multi dimensional cube in the data space, with equal volume cells. It is characterized by the following advantages.

First, NDF (p) can be obtained instantly by simply counting the number of points falling into the cell to which p belongs, without the involvement of any indexing techniques. Second, the dense regions can be efficiently identified, thus the computation of K_DF (p) can be very fast. Finally, based on the density of grid cells, to select the top n outliers only from a specified number of points viewed as outlier candidates, rather than the whole dataset and the final top n outliers are selected from these outlier candidates based on the ranking of their ODF values.

The major advantage of distance based algorithms is that, unlike distribution based methods, distance based methods are non parametric and do not rely on any assumed distribution to fit the data. The distance based definitions of outliers are fairly straightforward and easy to understand and implement. The major drawback is that most of them are not effective in high dimensional space due to the curse of dimensionality, though one is able to mechanically extend the distance metric such as Euclidean distance for high dimensional data.

The high dimensional data in real applications are very noisy and the abnormal deviations may be embedded in some lower dimensional subspaces that cannot be observed in the full data space. The definitions of a local neighborhood, irrespective of the circular neighborhood or the k nearest neighbors do not make much sense in high dimensional space. Since each point tends to be equidistant with each other as number of dimensions goes up, the degree of outlier-ness of each points are approximately identical and significant phenomenon of deviation or abnormality cannot be observed. Thus, none of the data points can be viewed outliers if the concepts of proximity are used to define outliers. In addition, neighborhood and k-NN search in high dimensional space [Augusteijn M and Folkert B, 2002] is a non-trivial and expensive task.

Straightforward algorithms, such as those based on nested loops, typically require $O(n^2)$ distance computations. This quadratic scaling means that it will be very difficult to mine outliers as tackle increasingly larger data sets. This is a major problem for many real databases where there are often millions of records. Thus, these approaches lack a good scalability for large data set. Finally, the existing distance based methods are not able to deal with data streams due to the difficulty in maintaining a data distribution in the local neighborhood or finding the k-NN for the data in the stream.

The distance based approach detect as follows. Given a distance measure on a feature space, a point q in a data set is an outlier with respect to the parameters m and d, if there are less than m points within the distance d from q, where the values of m and d are decided by the user. The problem with this approach is that it is difficult to determine the values of m and d [Ramaswami S, 2000; Angiulli F and Pizzuti C, 2005].

4.3.5. Density Based Methods

Density based methods use more complex mechanisms to model the outlier ness of data points than distance based methods. It usually involves investigating not only the local density of the point being studied but also the local densities of its nearest neighbors. Thus, the outlier-ness metric of a data point is relative in the sense that it is normally a ratio of density of this point against the averaged densities of its nearest neighbors. The major density based methods are Local Outlier Factor (LOF) method [Jianhao Tan and Jing Zhang, 2010], Connectivity Based Outlier Factor (COF) method, Influenced Outlier-ness (INFLO) method [Pokrajac D et al., 2007] and Multi Granularity Deviation Factor (MGDF) method.

4.3.5.1. Local Outlier Factor (LOF) Method

The first major density based formulation scheme of outlier has been proposed Breunig M, et al., [2000] which is more robust than the distance based outlier detection methods. The dataset contains an outlier o, and c1 and c2 are two clusters with different densities. The DB (k, λ) outlier method cannot distinguish o from the rest of the dataset no matter the values of the parameters k and λ taken. This is because the density of o's neighborhood is very much closer to that of the points in cluster c1. However, the density based method has been proposed [Breunig M, et al., 2000] to handle it successfully. This density based formulation quantifies the outlying degree of points using Local Outlier Factor (LOF). Given parameter MinPts, LOF of a point p is defined as

$$LOF_{Minpts(p)} = \sum_{o \in Minpts(p)} ((lrd_{minpts}(o) / lrd_{minpts}(p)) / |N_{minpts}(p)|$$

where $|N_{MinPts}(p)|$ denotes the number of objects falling into the MinPts-neighborhood of p and $lrd_{MinPts}(p)$ denotes the local reachability density of point p that is defined as the inverse of the average reachability distance based on the MinPts nearest neighbors of p. Further, the reach ability distance of point p is defined as reach distMinPts (p, o) = max (MinPts distance (o), dist (p, o)) intuitively speaking, LOF of an object reflects the density contrast between its density and those of its neighborhood. The neighborhood is defined by the distance to the MinPtsth nearest neighbor. The local outlier factor is a mean value of the ratio of the density distribution estimate in the neighborhood of the object analyzed to the distribution densities of its neighbors. The lower the density of p and/or the higher the densities of p's neighbors, the larger the value of LOF (p), which indicates that p has a higher degree of being an outlier. Unfortunately, the LOF method requires the computation of LOF for all objects in the data set which is rather expensive because it requires a large number of k-NN searches. The high cost of computing LOF for each data point p is caused by two factors [Zhou S et al., 2005].

First, to find the MinPtsth nearest neighbor of p in order to specify its neighborhood. This resembles to computing D^k in detecting D^n outliers. Second, after the MinPtsth neighborhood of p has been determined, find the MinPtsth neighborhood for each data points falling into the MinPtsth neighborhood of p. This amounts to MinPtsth times in terms of computation efforts as computing D^k when detecting D^n_k outliers. It is desired to constrain a search to only the top n outliers instead of computing the LOF of every object in the database. The efficiency of this algorithm is boosted by an efficient micro cluster based local outlier mining algorithm. LOF ranks points by only considering the neighborhood density of the points, thus it may miss out the potential outliers whose densities are close to those of their neighbors. Furthermore, the effectiveness of this algorithm using LOF is rather sensitive to the choice of MinPts, the parameter used to specify the local neighborhood.

4.3.5.2. Connectivity Based Outlier Factor (COF) Method

As LOF method suffers the drawback that it may miss those potential outliers whose local neighborhood density is very close to that of its neighbors. The Connectivity based Outlier Factor (COF) [Teng H et al., 2012] scheme that improves the effectiveness of LOF scheme when a pattern itself has similar neighborhood density as an outlier. In order to model the connectivity of a data point with respect to a group of its neighbors, a Set Based Nearest path (SBN path) and further a Set Based Nearest trail (SBN trail), originated from this data points are defined [Forrest S et al., 1996]. This SBN trail stating from a point is considered to be the pattern presented by the neighbors of this point. Based on SBN trail, the cost of this trail, a weighted sum of the cost of all its constituting edges, is computed.

$$COF_{K(p)} = |N_{K(p)}| \cdot ac\_distN_{k(p)}(p) / \sum_{o \varepsilon Nk(p)} ac\_distN_{k(o)}(o)$$

where $distN_{k(p)}(p)$ is the average chaining distance from point p to the rest of this k nearest neighbors which is the weighted sum of the cost of SBN trail starting from p. The COF method is able to detect outlier more effectively than LOF method for some cases. However, COF method requires more expensive computations than LOF and the time complexity is in the order of O (n^2) for high dimensional datasets.

4.3.5.3. Influenced Outlier-Ness (INFLO) Method

Even though LOF is able to accurately estimate outlier-ness of data points in most cases, it fails to do so in some complicated situations. For instance, when outliers are in the location where the density distributions in the neighborhood are significantly different, this may result in a wrong estimation. LOF is due to the inaccurate specification of the space where LOF is applied. To solve this problem of LOF an improved method, called INFLO is used.

INFLO is very similar to LOF. With respect to a data point p, they are both defined as the ratio of p's its density and the average density of its neighboring objects. However, INFLO uses only the data points in its k influence space for calculating the density ratio. Using INFLO, the densities of its neighborhood will be reasonably estimated and thus the outliers found will be more meaningful. The idea of INFLO is that both the nearest neighbors (NNs) and Reverse Nearest Neighbors (RNNs) of a data point are taken into account in order to get a better estimation of the neighborhood's density distribution. The RNNs of an object p are those data points that have p as one of their k nearest neighbors. By considering the symmetric neighborhood relationship of both NN and RNN, the space of an object influenced by other objects is well determined. This space is called the k influence space of a data point. The outlier-ness of a data point, called INFLuenced Outlier ness (INFLO) is quantified.

4.3.5.4. Multi Granularity Deviation Factor (MGDF) Method

Intuitively, the MGEF at radius r for a point p_i is the relative deviation of its local neighborhood density from the average local neighborhood density in its r neighborhood. Let n (p_i, α_r) be the number of objects in the α_r-neighborhood of p_i and n (p_i, r, α) be the average, over all objects p in the r neighborhood of p_i, of n (p, αr) [Theiler J and Cai D.M, 2003]. MDEF of p_i, given r and α, is defined as

$$MDEF(p_i, r, \alpha) = 1 - (n(p_i, ar) / n (p_i, r, a))$$

The density based outlier detection methods are generally more effective than the distance based methods. However, in order to achieve the improved effectiveness, the density based methods are more complicated and computationally expensive. For a data object, not only explore its local density but also that of its neighbors. Expensive k-NN search is expected for all the existing methods in this category. Due to the inherent complexity and non-updatability of their outlier-ness measurements used LOF, COF, INFLO and MDEF cannot handle data streams efficiently [Breunig M et al., 2000].

In Table 4.1 describes the comparison of outlier detection in various methods [Ji Zhan, 2013]. In this table, evaluate each method against two criteria, namely whether it can detect projected outliers in a high-dimensional data space and whether it can handle datastreams. The symbol of yes and no in the table indicate respectively whether or not the corresponding method satisfies the evaluation criteria. From this table, that the conventional outlier detection methods cannot detect projected outliers embedded in different subspaces to detect outliers only in the full data space or a given subspace. Regression models, Histogram models, Kernal models and Incremental LOF can handle datastream.

Table 4.1: Comparison of Outlier Detection Approaches [Ji Zhan, 2013]

Category	Method	High-D outlier	Data Stream
Statistical based Methods	Gaussian Models	No	No
	Regression Models	No	Yes
	Histogram Models	No	Yes
	Kernal Models	No	Yes
Distance based methods	Db(k,λ)-outliers	No	No
	Db(pct,dmin)-outliers	No	No
	k-NN Method	No	No
	Grid-ODF	No	No
Density based methods	LOF	No	No
	COF	No	No
	INFLO	No	No
	MDEF	No	No
	Incremental LOF	No	Yes

4.4.   Outlier Detection Tools

Outlier detection tools are support vector machines, Bayesian network based, Neural network based, regression models, clustering, nearest neighboring techniques and mixture of parametric models.

4.4.1. Support Vector Machines

Support Vector Machines (SVMs) [Davy M and Godsill S, 2002] is a machine learning paradigm which is principally used as a binary classification tool. The SVM separates the data belonging to different classes by fitting a hyper plane between them which maximizes the separation.

The performance of an SVM depends on the data separation. To overcome this, the data is mapped to a higher dimensional feature space where it can be easily separated by a hyper plane. But since finding the hyper plane requires the inner products between the vectors, explicit mapping is not essential. Instead a kernel function is used to approximate the dot product between the mapped vectors.

The SVMs are applied for outlier detection in supervised mode [Steinwart I et al., 2005]. An unsupervised learning based technique which tries to learn the high density and the low density regions of data. Assuming that normal instances belong to the high density region, outliers belong to the low density region. The testing phase classes a test instance to one of these two classes and accordingly declares the instance as normal or outlying. The density level detection is being done by using a Support Vector Machine. The SVM has been applied to outlier detection by adapting them for single class classification (semi supervised learning). Thus an intuitive technique would be to draw the smallest hyper sphere which contains all points belonging to the normal class. Testing would simply involve determining which side of that hyper sphere a test point lies. Similar implementations are proposed for outlier detection in audio signal data [Davy M and Godsill, 2002], novelty detection in power generation plants [King S et al., 2002] and system call intrusion detection [Eskin et al., 2002; Song Q et al., 2002] extend the one class SVM for outlier detection in temporal sequences. In this technique, matching function define to determine match by a test sequence match.

The matching function is denoted as $F (M_x (t_o, 1), x (t_o))$, is a function that can quantify how well the model $M_x (t_0)$ matches the temporal sequence. Another variant of the above approach [Monson G et al., 2000; Song Q et al., 2002] tries to separate the regions containing data from the regions containing no data.

The primary assumption here is that the training data should be purely normal. Thus the classifier obtained is a binary classifier which outputs +1 if the test instance falls inside one of the regions containing data and outputs -1 if the test instance falls inside one of the regions containing no data points.

4.4.2. Bayesian Network Based

A typical Bayesian network used for outlier detection aggregates information from different variables and provides an estimate on the expectancy of that event to belong to the normal classes [Kruegel C et al., 2003]. Thus, the training phase creates a tree type structure where all child nodes are the variables (measuring the properties of the event) which feed the value to one root node for aggregation and classification of the event as normal or outlier. Naive Bayesian networks are used to incorporate prior probabilities into a reasoning model which then classifies an event as normal or outlier based on the observed properties of the event and the prior probabilities [Keogh et al., 2002; Keogh et al., 2006].

Bayesian networks are used to augment the capabilities of an existing statistical or any other outlier detection system. Bayesian nets are also used to create models of attack patterns along with the model of normal behavior. This approach prevents a system to "learn" an attack pattern as normal behavior. Similarly Kruegel C et al., [2003] used a Bayesian network to models the causal dependencies between the different properties of the event and also any external knowledge about the measured properties to classify any event as normal or outlier. Pseudo Bayes estimators are used to reduce the false alarm rate of an outlier detection system [Barbara D et al., 2001]. The system learns the prior and posterior probabilities of unseen attacks from the training data. The instances classified as outliers by the system and then classified as "normal" or "new attacks" using the Naive Bayes classifier [Bronstein A et al., 2001].

A Denial of Service (DOS) attack detection technique based on the Dempster's-Shafer's Theory of Evidence involves data fusion from multiple sensors to obtain posterior probabilities and then using Bayesian inference to estimate probability of an event in the monitored network [Siaterlis C and Maglaris B, 2004].

4.4.3. Neural Networks

Neural Networks [Jakubek S and Strasser T, 2002] are widely used for building classifiers by learning different weights associated with the network. When a test instance fed into this neural network may produce one of the output nodes as the output (determining the class of the test instance) or no output (determining that the test instance does not belong to any of the learnt classes). Neural networks have been extensively used for novelty detection [Markou M and Singh S, 2003; Ghosh S and Reilly D.L, 2012]. The basic idea is to train the neural network on the normal training data and then detect novelties by analyzing the response of the trained neural network to a test input. If the network accepts a test input, it is normal and if the network rejects a test input, it is an outlier [Dorronsoro J.R et al., 1997].

4.4.4. Regression Models

Outlier detection using regression has been extensively investigated for time series.

Two types of outliers in time series data have been identified.

- Observational outliers - These occur when a single observation is extreme.
- Innovational outliers - These occur when an "innovation" at an instance is extreme which affects the observation at that instance as well as the subsequent observations.

The primary approach for detecting outliers in time series data has been using regression analysis. The training phase involves fitting a regression model on the data. The testing phase is essentially a model diagnostics phase which involves evaluating each instance with respect to the model.

The maximum likelihood estimates of the regression parameters are used as the criteria for outlier detection. The underlying approach in these techniques is to fit a regression model on the time series and estimate certain statistics which are diagnosed to detect outliers in the time series. Some statisticians argue that using such significance test is not always the best approach to detect outliers.

4.4.5. Clustering Tool

Cluster analysis is a popular machine learning technique to group similar data instances into clusters. It is either used as a standalone tool to get insight into the distribution of a data set, e.g. to focus further analysis and data processing or as a preprocessing step for other algorithms operating on the detected clusters. Clustering is primarily an unsupervised technique though semi supervised clustering has also been explored lately. Clustering and outlier detection appear to be fundamentally very different from each other. While the former aims at detecting groups with similar behavior the later aims at detecting instances which are not similar to any other instances in the data. But clustering based outlier detection techniques have been developed which make use of the fact that outliers do not belong to any cluster since they are very few and different from the normal instances [Nairac A et al., 1997].

The clustering based techniques involve clustering steps which partition the data into groups which contain similar objects. The assumed behavior of outliers is that they either does not belong to any cluster or belong to very small clusters or forced to belong to a cluster where they are very different from other members. Similarly, the normal instances belong to dense and large clusters. This distinction makes it possible to separate out the outliers from the rest of the data.

The advantage of the cluster based schemes is that do not have to be supervised. Moreover, clustering based schemes are capable of being used in an incremental mode i.e. after learning the clusters, new points can be fed in to the system and tested for outliers. One disadvantage of clustering based approaches is that they are computationally expensive.

4.4.6. *Nearest Neighboring Techniques*

Nearest neighbor analysis is a widely used concept in machine learning and data mining in which a data object is analyzed with respect to its nearest neighbors [Sun J et al., 2009]. This concept has been applied for different purposes such as classification, clustering and also outlier detection. The salient feature of nearest neighbor based outlier detection tool is that they have an explicit notion of proximity, defined in the form of a distance or similarity measure for any two individual data instances, or a set of instances or a sequence of instances [Theiler J and Cai D.M., 2003]. These approaches typically map the data instances in a metric space defined over a finite number of features. While clustering based schemes take a global view of the data, nearest neighbor based schemes analysis each object with respect to its local neighborhood. The basic idea behind such schemes is that an outlier has a neighborhood where it stand out, while a normal object has a neighborhood where all its neighbors exactly like it. The obvious strength of these techniques is that they can work in an unsupervised mode, i.e. they do not assume availability of class labels.

4.4.7. *Mixture of Parametric Models*

In several scenarios single statistical models are not sufficient to represent the data and in such cases a mixture of parametric models are used and these techniques can work in two ways. First approach is supervised and involves modeling the normal instances and outliers as separate parametric distributions. The testing phase would involve determining which distribution the test instance belongs to. The second approach is semi supervised and involves modeling the normal instances as a mixture of models. For instance a test which does not belong to any of the learnt models is declared to be outlier. Simplest application of the first approach is when both normal instances and outliers are modeled separately.

Expectation Maximization (EM) algorithm is used to develop a mixture of models for the two classes, assuming that each data point is an outlier with a probability λ and normal with a probability 1- λ. Thus, if D represents the actual probability distribution of the entire data and M and A represent the distributions of the normal and anomalous data respectively, then D = λ A + (1 - λ) M. M is learnt, using any machine learning technique while A is assumed to be uniform. Initially all points are considered to be in M. The anomaly score [Surace C et al., 1997] is assigned to a point based on how much the distributions change if that point is removed from M and added to A.

A similar approach is adopted for novel event detection in text documents [King S et al., 2002]. Each of the known normal classes is assumed to be generated by some parametric model. These parameters are estimated using EM. For sparse classes, the authors adopt a technique called hierarchical shrinkage to estimate the parameters. The outlier detection is essentially a Bayesian classification task, where depending on the test document the authors predict if it belongs to a normal class or a novel class.

Table 4.2: Comparison of the Outlier Detection (%) [Agyemang M et al., 2006]

(%)Approach	Outlier Detection (%)
Distance based approach	28
Statistical based approach	65
Density based approach	81

In Table 4.2 describes the three classical outlier detection methods have been applied to the database: a distance based approach, density based approach and statistical based approach. The distance based approach is capable to point out the outliers that mostly differ from the mean value, while the density based approach detects only outliers that are isolated from data. Finally the statistical based approach considers as outliers those points that deviate from the model. In this example, the density based approach better than other two approaches.

4.5.   Outlier Applications

A more exhaustive list of applications that utilize outlier detection is:

- Fraud detection [Barson P et al., 1996; Cox K.C et al., 1997]-Detecting fraudulent applications for credit cards, state benefits or detecting fraudulent usage of credit cards or mobile phones.
- Loan application processing-Detecting fraudulent applications or potentially problematical customers.
- Intrusion detection - Detecting unauthorized access in computer networks.
- Activity monitoring [Fawcett T and Provost F, 1999] - Detecting mobile phone fraud by monitoring phone activity or suspicious trades in the equity markets.
- Network performance [Augusteijn M and Folkert B, 2002] - Monitoring the performance of computer networks, for example to detect network bottlenecks.
- Fault diagnosis - Monitoring processes to detect faults in motors, generators, pipelines or space instruments on space shuttles for example.

- Structural defect detection - Monitoring manufacturing lines to detect faulty production runs for example cracked beams.
- Satellite image analysis [Blender R et al., 1997] - Identifying novel features or misclassified features.
- Detecting novelties in images [Albrecht S et al., 2000] - For robot surveillance systems.
- Motion segmentation - Detecting image features moving independently of the background.
- Time series monitoring - Monitoring safety critical applications such as drilling or high speed milling.
- Medical condition monitoring - Such as heart rate monitors.
- Pharmaceutical research - Identifying novel molecular structures.
- Detecting novelty in text [Campbell C and Bennett K, 2001] - Detecting the onset of news stories for topic detection and tracking or for traders to pinpoint equity, commodities, FX trading stories, outperforming or underperforming commodities.
- Detecting unexpected entries in databases - For data mining to detect errors, frauds or valid but unexpected entries.
- Detecting mislabeled data in a training data set.

4.6.   Domain of Outlier Detection

Outlier detection techniques in this domain primarily detect novel topics or events or news stories in a collection of documents or news articles. The outliers are caused due to a new interesting event or an anomalous topic.

4.6.1.   *Outlier Detection in Text Data*

The data in this domain is typically high dimensional and very sparse. The data also has a temporal aspect since the documents are collected over time. A challenge for outlier detection techniques in this domain is to handle the large variations in documents belonging to one category or topic.

4.6.2.   *Outlier Detection in Image*

Outlier detection aims to detect changes in an image over time (motion detection) or in regions which appear abnormal on the static image. This domain includes satellite image [Singh S and Markou M, 2009], digit recognition, spectroscopy, mammography image and video surveillance. The outliers are caused by motion or insertion of foreign object or instrumentation errors. The data has spatial as well as temporal characteristics. Each data point has a few continuous attributes such as color, lightness, texture, etc. The interesting outliers are either anomalous points or regions in the images (point and contextual outliers). One of the key challenges in this domain is the large size of the input. The challenge is greater when dealing with video data and online detection techniques are required.

4.7. Discussion

The literature survey shows that outliers are difficult to identify in diverse fields and application domain of research. Literature on this work can be broadly classified into three major categories based on the techniques used i.e., statistical approach, distance based approach and density based approach which are discussed in this chapter. From the above discussion, the statistical approach is rather limited to large real world databases which typically have many different fields and it is not easy to characterize the multivariate distribution of exemplars.

The major drawback of distance based approach is that most of them are not effective in high dimensional space due to the curse of dimensionality, though one is able to mechanically extend the distance metric such as Euclidean distance for high dimensional data.

The density based outlier detection approach is generally more effective than the distance based approach. However, in order to achieve the improved effectiveness, the density based approach is more complicated and computationally expensive. Density based approaches have been proved to be effective in detecting outliers successfully, but usually requires huge amount of computations. The density based approach of the proposed research is to find outlier of image effectively by improving cluster quality.

Review Questions

1. What are point outliers? Explain.
2. Briefly explain the Contextual Outlier attributes?
3. Discuss about the outlier detection methods in detail.
4. Differentiate the single step and sequential procedures.
5. What is multivariate outlier detection methods and explain with neat diagram.
6. Explain about the Gaussian models in detail.
7. How to implement the local neighborhood method in distance based outliers.

CHAPTER IV

TRENDS IN DATA MINING

5.1. Applications and Trends in Data Mining

"What are some specific examples of the use of data mining for applications in science and business? Where will data mining be in the future?" Here discuss data mining applications and provide tips on what to consider when purchasing a data mining software system. Additional themes in data mining are described, such as visual and audio mining, statistical techniques for data mining and theoretical foundations of data mining and intelligent query answering by the incorporation of data mining techniques. The social impacts of data mining and future trends are also discussed.

5.2. Current Trends

The field of data mining has been growing due to its enormous success in terms of broad-ranging application achievements and scientific progress understanding. Various data mining applications have been successfully implemented in various domains like health care, finance, retail, telecommunication, fraud detection and risk analysis etc. The ever increasing complexities in various fields and improvements in technology have posed new challenges to data mining; the various challenges include different data formats, data from disparate locations, advances in computation and networking resources, research and scientific fields, ever growing business challenges etc. Advancements in data mining with various integrations and implications of methods and techniques have shaped the present data mining applications to handle the various challenges, the current trends of data mining applications are:

5.3. Future Trends

Due to the enormous success of various application areas of data mining, the field of data mining has been establishing itself as the major discipline of computer science and has shown interest potential for the future developments. Ever increasing technology and future application areas are always poses new challenges and opportunities for data mining, the typical future trends of data mining includes:

- Standardization of data mining languages
- Data preprocessing
- Complex objects of data

- Computing resources
- Web mining
- Scientific Computing
- Business data

5.4. Data Mining Applications

Since data mining is a young discipline with wide and diverse applications, there is still a nontrivial gap between general principles of data mining and domain-specific, effective data mining tools for particular applications. In this section, examine a few application domains and discuss how customized data mining tools should be developed for such applications.

Data Trends

In initial days, data mining algorithms work best for numerical data collected from a single data base, and various data mining techniques have evolved for flat files, traditional and relational databases where the data is stored in tabular representation. Later on, with the confluence of Statistics and Machine Learning techniques, various algorithms evolved to mine the non-numerical data and relational databases.

Audio Data Mining

Uses audio signals to indicate the patterns of data or the features of data mining results. Although visual data mining may disclose interesting patterns using graphical displays, it requires users to concentrate on watching patterns and identifying interesting or novel features within them. This can sometimes be quite tiresome. If patterns can be transformed into sound and music, then instead of watching pictures, listen to pitches, rhythms, tune, and melody in order to identify anything interesting or unusual. This may relieve some of the burden of visual concentration and be more relaxing than visual mining in many cases. Therefore, audio data mining can be an interesting alternative to visual mining.

Computing Trends

The field of data mining has been greatly influenced by the development of fourth generation programming languages and various related computing techniques. In, early days of data mining most of the algorithms employed only statistical techniques. Later on they evolved with various computing techniques like AI, ML and Pattern Reorganization. Various data mining techniques (Induction, Compression and Approximation) and algorithms developed to mine the large volumes of heterogeneous data stored in the data warehouses.

5.5.   Data Mining in Banks and Financial Institutions

Both public and private sector banks are heavily using Data mining for prediction of credit frauds, risk evaluation, credit rating, loan approval, profitability,detection of money laundering etc. In the financial markets, data mining techniques as decision trees and neural networks are used by financial analysts in portfolio management, mergers and acquisitions, forecasting financial crisis, bond rating, commodity price predictions etc (Langdell, 2010).

Data Mining in Surveillance of Corporate

Data mining is used as a Business Intelligence (BI) tool to enable corporate in optimized tailoring their products and services as desired and demanded by their customers. It creates pressure on members of target organization to act as informants. It is also applied in identifying terrorist activities of communication and financial transfers for example-Multistate Anti-Terrorism Information Exchange (MATRIX).

Data Mining in Telecommunication

Telecommunication sector has diverse pool of data in form of call data, network data and customer data. Thus to detect network faults and do analysis from this huge repository, data mining is used in telecommunication sector to support multidimensional analysis, identification of unusual patterns, sequential pattern analysis, fraudulent pattern analysis, visualization, customer profiling, marketing and network fault isolation.

Data Mining in Medical and Healthcare Sector

Data mining is used in healthcare industries to analyze immense data of medical research, patient, staff and doctors records, biotech and medicines and compounds in pharmaceutical industry thus enabling discovery of relationship between diseases, research of new drugs, treatments effectiveness, genetic network analysis and market activities in drug delivery services. For example-Neuro medical systems used neural networks to perform Pap smear diagnostics.

5.6.   Data Mining in Science and Research

Through data mining, scientific data, in form of heterogeneous streams containing temporal and spatial data, can be analyzed at higher speeds incurring lower costs. There is a considerable shift now from "hypothesis formulation and test" to "collect and store data, make new hypothesis and confirm with data or experiments". It is now successfully applied in areas of genetics, bio informatics and medicine, electrical power engineering and educational research.

Standardization of Data Mining Languages

There are various data mining tools with different syntaxes, hence it is to be standardized for making convenient of the users. Data mining applications has to concentrate more in standardization of interaction languages and flexible user interactions.

Data Preprocessing

To identify useful novel patterns in distributed, large, complex and temporal data, data mining techniques has to evolve in various stages. The present techniques and algorithms of data preprocessing stage are not up to the mark compared with its significance in finding out the novel patterns of data. In future there is a great need of data mining applications with efficient data preprocessing techniques.

Complex Object of Data

Data mining is going to penetrate in all fields of human life; the presently available data mining techniques are restricted to mine the traditional forms of data only, and in future there is a potentiality for data mining techniques for complex data objects like high dimensional, high speed data streams, sequence, noise in the time series, graph, Multi-instance objects, Multi-represented objects and temporal data.

Computing Resources

The contemporary developments in high speed connectivity, parallel, distributed, grid and cloud computing has posed new challenges for data mining. The high speed internet connectivity has posed a great demand for novel and efficient data mining techniques to analyze the massive data which is captured of IP packets at high link speeds in order to detect the Denial of Service (DoS) and other types of attacks.

Distributed data mining applications demand new alternatives in different fields, such as discovery of universal strategy to configure a distributed data mining, data placement at different locations, scheduling, resource management, and transactional systems etc. New data mining techniques and tools are needed to facilitate seamless integration of various resources in grid based environment. Moreover, grid based data mining has to focus seriously to address the data privacy, security and governance. Cloud computing is a great area to be focused by data mining, as the Cloud computing is penetrating more and more in all ranges of business and scientific computing. Data mining techniques and applications are very much needed in cloud computing paradigm.

5.7.   Web Mining

The development of World Wide Web and its usage grows, it will continue to generate ever more content, structure, and usage data and the value of Web mining will keep increasing. Research needs to be done in developing the right set of Web metrics, and their measurement procedures, extracting process models from usage data, understanding how different parts of the process model impact various Web metrics of interest, how the process models change in response to various changes that are made-changing stimuli to the user, developing Web mining techniques to improve various other aspects of Web services, techniques to recognize known frauds and intrusion detection.

Scientific Computing

In recent years data mining has attracted the research in various scientific computing applications, due to its efficient analysis of data, discovering meaningful new correlations, patterns and trends with the help of various tools and techniques. More research has to be done in mining of scientific data in particular approaches for mining astronomical, biological, chemical, and fluid dynamical data analysis. The ubiquitous use of embedded systems in sensing and actuation environments plays major impending developments in scientific computing will require a new class of techniques capable of dynamic data analysis in faulty, distributed framework. The research in data mining requires more attention in ecological and environmental information analysis to utilize our natural environment and resources. Significant data mining research has to be done in molecular biology problems.

5.8.   Data Mining for Biomedical and DNA Data Analysis

The past decade has seen an explosive growth in biomedical research, ranging from the development of new pharmaceuticals and advances in cancer therapies to the identification and study of the human genome by discovering large-scale sequencing patterns and gene functions. Since a great deal of biomedical research has focused on DNA data analysis, study this application here. Recent research in DNA analysis has led to the discovery of genetic causes for many diseases and disabilities, as well as the discovery of new medicines and approaches for disease diagnosis, prevention, and treatment. An important focus in genome research is the study of DNA sequences since such sequences form the foundation of the genetic codes of all living organisms. All DNA sequences are comprised of four basic building blocks (called nucleotides): adenine (A), cytosine (C), guanine (G), and thymine (T).

These four nucleotides are combined to form long sequences or chains that resemble a twisted ladder. Human beings have around 100,000 genes. A gene is usually comprised of hundreds of individual nucleotides arranged in a particular order. There are almost an unlimited number of ways that the nucleotides can be ordered and sequenced to form distinct genes. It is challenging to identify particular gene sequence patterns that play roles in various diseases. Since many interesting sequential pattern analysis and similarity search techniques have been developed in data mining, data mining has become a powerful tool and contributes substantially to DNA analysis in the following ways.

Semantic Integration of Heterogeneous, Distributed Genome Databases

Due to the highly distributed, uncontrolled generation and use of a wide variety of DNA data, the semantic integration of such heterogeneous and wide variety of distributed genome databases becomes an important task for systematic DNA coordinated analysis of DNA databases. This has promoted the development of integrated data warehouses and distributed federated databases to store and manages the primary and derived genetic data. Data cleaning and data integration methods developed in data mining will help the integration of genetic data and the construction of data warehouses for genetic data analysis.

Similarity Search and Comparison among DNA Sequences

Studied similarity search methods in time-series data mining. One of the most important search problems in genetic analysis is similarity search and comparison among DNA sequences. Gene sequences isolated from diseased and healthy tissues can be compared to identify critical differences between the two classes of genes. This can be done by first retrieving the gene sequences from the two tissue classes, and then finding and comparing the frequently in the diseased samples than in the healthy samples might indicate the genetic factors of the disease; on the other hand, those occurring only more frequently in the healthy samples might indicate mechanisms that protect the body from the disease.

Notice that although genetic analysis requires similarity search, the technique needed here is quite different from that used for time-series data. For example, data transformation methods such as scaling, normalization, and window stitching, which are popularly used in the analysis of time-series data, is ineffective for genetic data since such data are nonnumeric data and the precise interconnections between different kinds of nucleotides play an important role in their function. On the other hand, the analysis of frequent sequential patterns is important in the analysis of similarity and dissimilarity in genetic sequences.

Association Analysis: Identification of Co-occurring Gene Sequences

Currently, many studies have focused on the comparison of one gene to another. However, most diseases are not triggered by a single gene but by a combination of genes acting together. Association analysis methods can be used to help determine the kinds of genes that are likely to co-occur in target samples. Such analysis would facilitate the discovery of groups of genes and the study of interactions and relationships between them.

Path Analysis: Linking Genes to Different Stages of Disease Development

While a group of genes may contribute to a disease process, different genes may become active at different stages of the disease. If the sequence of genetic activities across the different stages of disease development can be identified, it may be possible to develop pharmaceutical interventions that target the different stages separately, therefore achieving more effective treatment of the disease. Such path analysis is expected to play an important role in genetic studies.

Visualization Tools and Genetic Data Analysis

Complex structures and sequencing patterns of genes are most effectively presented in graphs, trees, cuboids, and chains by various kinds of visualization tools. Such visually appealing structures and patterns facilitate pattern understanding, knowledge discovery, and interactive data exploration. Visualization therefore plays an important role in biomedical data mining.

5.9. Data Mining for Financial Data Analysis

Most banks and financial institutions offer a wide variety of banking services (such as checking, savings, and business and individual customer transactions), credit (such as business, mortgage, and automobile loans), and investment services (such as mutual funds). Some also offer insurance services and stock investment services. Financial data collected in the banking and financial industries are often relatively completed, reliable, and of high quality, which facilitates systematic data analysis and data mining. Here present a few typical cases. Given databases of sufficient size and quality data mining technology can generate new business opportunities by providing these capabilities:

- **Automated prediction of trends and behaviors**. Data mining automates the process of finding predictive information in large databases. Questions that traditionally required extensive hands-on analysis can now be answered directly from the data — quickly. A typical example of a predictive problem is targeted marketing. Data mining uses data on past promotional mailings to identify the targets most likely to maximize return on investment in future mailings. Other predictive problems include forecasting bankruptcy and other forms of default, and identifying segments of a population likely to respond similarly to given events.

- **Automated discovery of previously unknown patterns**. Data mining tools sweep through databases and identify previously hidden patterns in one step. An example of pattern discovery is the analysis of retail sales data to identify seemingly unrelated products that are often purchased together. Other pattern discovery problems include detecting fraudulent credit card transactions and identifying anomalous data that could represent data entry keying errors.

The most commonly used techniques in data mining are:

- **Artificial neural networks**: Non-linear predictive models that learn through training and resemble biological neural networks in structure.
- **Decision trees**: Tree-shaped structures that represent sets of decisions. These decisions generate rules for the classification of a dataset. Specific decision tree methods include Classification and Regression Trees (CART) and Chi Square Automatic Interaction Detection (CHAID).
- **Genetic algorithms**: Optimization techniques that use process such as genetic combination, mutation, and natural selection in a design based on the concepts of evolution.
- **Nearest neighbor method**: A technique that classifies each record in a dataset based on a combination of the classes of the k record(s) most similar to it in a historical dataset (where $k^3 1$). Sometimes called the k-nearest neighbor technique.
- **Rule induction**: The extraction of useful if-then rules from data based on statistical significance.

Biological Data Analysis

Now a day, there is vast growth in field of biology such as genomics, proteomics, functional Genomics and biomedical research. Biological data mining is very important part of Bioinformatics. Following are the aspects in which Data mining contribute for biological data analysis:

- Semantic integration of heterogeneous, distributed genomic and proteomic databases.
- Alignment, indexing, similarity search and comparative analysis multiple nucleotide sequences.

- Discovery of structural patterns and analysis of genetic networks and protein pathways.
- Association and path analysis.
- Visualization tools in genetic data analysis.

5.10. Other Scientific Applications

The applications discussed above tend to handle relatively small and homogeneous data sets for which the statistical techniques are appropriate. Huge amount of data have been collected from scientific domains such as geosciences, astronomy etc. There is large amount of data sets being generated because of the fast numerical simulations in various fields such as climate, and ecosystem modeling, chemical engineering, fluid dynamics etc. Following are the applications of data mining in field of Scientific Applications:

- Data Warehouses and data preprocessing.
- Graph-based mining.
- Visualization and domain specific knowledge.

Intrusion Detection

Intrusion refers to any kind of action that threatens integrity, confidentiality, or availability of network resources. In this world of connectivity security has become the major issue. With increased usage of internet and availability of tools and tricks for intruding and attacking network prompted intrusion detection to become a critical component of network administration. Here is the list of areas in which data mining technology may be applied for intrusion detection:

- Development of data mining algorithm for intrusion detection.
- Association and correlation analysis, aggregation to help select and build discriminating attributes.
- Analysis of Stream data.
- Distributed data mining.
- Visualization and query tools.

Trends in Data Mining Here is the list of trends in data mining that reflects pursuit of the challenges such as construction of integrated and interactive data mining environments, design of data mining languages:

- Application Exploration
- Scalable and Interactive data mining methods

- Integration of data mining with database systems, data warehouse systems and web database systems.
- Standardization of data mining query language
- Visual Data Mining
- New methods for mining complex types of data
- Biological data mining
- Data mining and software engineering
- Web mining
- Distributed Data mining
- Real time data mining
- Multi Database data mining
- privacy protection and Information Security in data mining

Database Security

In an ethical sense, database security is related to privacy. This is because database security inhibits the unauthorized dissemination of personal data thus further enhancing, albeit indirectly, an individual's capacity to regulate access to their data. In terms of database security, two forms of KD operation need to be considered: those operating as authorized applications by an individual or organization that holds and has full access to the data; and · those operating as unauthorized applications by an individual or organization that has access to the data only insomuch as has been permitted for other allowable purposes. Note that the individual need not be external to the organization that holds the data for the second operation to occur.

Conventional database security protects data via user authorization techniques (O'Leary 1991) making no distinction between the degrees of sensitivity present in the database (Mills 1997). A more sophisticated model, Multi Level Security (MLS) extends conventional security measures by classifying data according to its confidentiality (Elmasri and Navathe 1994). The data in an MLS database is typically sorted into four security levels, with users permitted access only to their authorized level. This increases the protection of data from misuse by both authorized and unauthorized users.

Encryption is another popular database security technique. This approach has been offered commercially in updates to Oracle8i (Hammond 2000) which encrypt individual data items. Encryption is considered particularly applicable to databases accessible via the web, because of the increased data exposure and vulnerability inherent to this means of data access. It is not an infallible data security technique and a brief search of the literature will reveal numerous instances where data encryption has been insufficient. Finally, auditing (Austin 1999) is used to record databases transactions and who executed them. It is commonly used as a tool for enhancing database performance (Johnson 1999), as it identifies the busiest tables, privileges, etc but it can also be used to identify attempted database intrusions. However, auditing provides historical data for analysis rather than a means of detecting database intrusion as it occurs and its value as a preventative security measure is minimal. Miller (1991) showed how users executing specific queries at their authorized security level in an MLS database could easily infer more sensitive information and later Thuraisingham (1997) discussed the possibility of this occurring during DM. There exists a set of precautions that can enhance existing database security to improve the protection of personal data from unauthorized KD applications. Firstly, restricting mining applications to one security level in an MLS database can inhibit inference from less sensitive data to more sensitive data (Lin, Hinke, Marks and Thuraisingham 1996). Secondly, the introduction of noise to the data serves to corrupt the results of any symbolic learning techniques present in a DM tool (Miller 1991, O'Leary 1991). Finally, the introduction of instability to the data (O'Leary 1991) renders it unsuitable for mining by hindering the extraction of meaningful information. Note that these measures are reversible for authorized applications.

The combination of these precautions with conventional database security models only serves to discourage unauthorized KD by rendering it a complex and cost intensive exercise. Means of ensuring infallible protection of data from malicious applications are yet to emerge.

Data Accuracy

The paper previously noted the OECDÕs guidelines (1980) for protecting personal data. One of the guidelines requires personal data to be precise, complete, and current in order to protect people from the harmful repercussions associated with poor data quality. This becomes all the more relevant when a KD application reveals information with detrimental repercussions for a data subject, especially as information is customarily taken as infallible regardless of whether it is in fact true or false (Gavison 1984).

Knowledge Discovery applications involve vast amounts of data, which are likely to have originated from many diverse, possibly external, sources. This means the initial quality of the data cannot be assured and it might be noisy, obsolete, inaccurate, or incomplete (Cavoukian 1998). Moreover, although data pre-processing (or cleaning) is undertaken before a mining application to improve data quality, people conduct transactions in a sporadic and largely unpredictable manner, which causes personal data to expire rapidly. In some cases, what is accurate data in one point in time is inaccurate shortly after that. When a KD application is executed over expired data inaccurate patterns are more likely to emerge, which can lead to negative consequences for an individual.

5.11. The Research Dilemma

When conducting research, well documented and clearly defined ethical guidelines should be followed by those interested in the integrity of their work. One example of such guidelines is the Australian Joint NHMRC/AVCC Statement and Guidelines on Research Practice (1997). This document presents ethical strategies for data storage and retention, authorship, publication, supervision of students and research trainees, disclosure of potential conflicts of interest, and research misconduct. It is intended to provide a national basis for Australian research institutions ethics policies. Accordingly, Australian University research policies (see for example the University of South Australia's Council Policies-Research (1997)) cover human research procedures, genetic manipulation and recombinant DNA research, animal experimentation, radiation safety, biohazards, and responsible research practice (as outlined by the Office of National Health and Medical Research Council (1997)). However, while these documents thoroughly consider the practical issues immediately associated with research, they both fail to consider the sociological influence of research results generally, and of emerging information technologies in particular.

The term Disruptive technologies has been coined by business researchers (Christensen 1997) to refer to technologies that have an agitating effect on a market and the organizations competing within it. How it is this term has not been adapted by sociologists and computer scientists to describe technologies that disrupt our cultures? Examples of such technologies abound. A perusal of any computer ethics text (for example Baase (1997)) will reveal discourse regarding software accidents, risks, crime, hacking, and so on. However, these discussions typically cite documented incidents and fail to identify the possibility of evaluating a technology's potential for social disruption.

In 1965, Einstein lamented the impact of his research on humanity:

The release of atomic power has changed everything except our way of thinking...the solution to this problem lies in the heart of mankind. If only I had known, I should have become a watchmaker.

Later, Weizenbaum (1972) discussed the responsibility of the computer scientist to their society. He called for the recognition of social responsibility by computer scientists and considered the computer scientist ultimately responsible for the impact of his/her research.

However, argue that while the computer scientist's thorough understanding of their work provides them with the capacity to argue on the work's behalf, it does not provide the capacity to estimate the work's social impact. Only a combination of suitably qualified individuals, historical information, and a comprehensive understanding of the emerging technology can adequately provide such an estimate. In the UK, the problem is being addressed by the Foundation for Information Policy Research (1999), an independent organization examining the interaction between information technology and society:

Our goal is to identify technical developments with significant social impact, commission research into public policy alternatives, and promote public understanding and dialogue between technologists and policy-makers in the UK and Europe.

It combines information technology researchers with people interested in social impacts, and uses a strong media presence to disseminate its arguments and educate the public. The involvement of diversely qualified people, the consideration given to each emerging technology, and the active dissemination policy, clearly provides an effective method of assessing the cultural impact of technological developments.

Review Questions

1. Explain the current trend in data mining.
2. What is Audio data mining? Explain.
3. How the data mining helps in the Banks and Financial Institutions? Explain.
4. What is role of Data Mining in Medical and Healthcare Sector?
5. Discuss the Data Mining in Science and Research.
6. Data Mining for Biomedical and DNA Data Analysis-How?
7. How data mining helps for Intrusion Detection in network? Explain.

References

1.   E. Acuna and C. Rodriguez, "A meta analysis study of outlier detection methods in classification", Technical paper, Department of Mathematics, University of Puerto Rico at Mayaguez, Proceedings IPSI, Venice, 2004.

2.   C.C. Aggarwal and P.S. Yu, "Outlier Detection for High Dimensional Data", Proceedings of the ACM SIGMOD Conference, 2001.

3.   M. Agyemang, K. Barker and R. Alhajj, "A comprehensive survey of numeric and symbolic outlier mining techniques", Intelligent Data Analysis, Vol.10, No.6, Pp.521-538, 2006.

4.   S. Albrecht, J. Busch, M. Kloppenburg, F. Metze and P. Tavan, "Generalized radial basis function networks for classification and novelty detection: self organization of optional Bayesian decision", Neural Networks, Vol.13, No.10, Pp.1075-1093, 2000.

5.   E. Aleskerov, B. Freisleben and R.B. Cardwatch, "A neural network based database mining system for credit card fraud detection", Proceedings of IEEE Computational Intelligence for Financial Engineering, Pp.220-226, 1997.

6.   Anant Ram, Sunita Jalal, Anand S. Jalal and Manoj kumar, "A density Based Algorithm for Discovery Density Varied cluster in Large spatial Databases", International Journal of Computer Application, Vol. 3, No.6, 2010.

7.   F. Angiulli and F. Fassetti, "Detecting Distance-based Outliers in Streams of Data", Proceedings of CIKM'07, Pp.811-820, 2007.

8.   F. Angiulli and C. Pizzuti, "Outlier mining in large high-dimensional data sets", IEEE Trans. Knowl. Data Eng., Vol.17, No.2, Pp.203-215, 2005.

9.   M. Ankerst, M.M. Breunig, H.P. Kriegel and J. Sander, "Optics: Ordering points to identify the clustering structure", Proceedings SIGMOD'99, Pp.49-60, 1999.

10.   Annan Naidu Paidi, "Data Mining: Future Trends and Applications", International Journal Of Modern Engineering Research, Vol.2, No.6, Pp:4657-4663, 2012.

11.   F.J. Anscombe and I. Guttman, "Rejection of outliers", Techno metrics, Vol.2, No.2, 1960.

12.   A. Arning, R. Agrawal and P. Raghavan, "A linear method for deviation detection in large databases", Proceedings of Knowledge Discovery and Data Mining, 1996.

13.   M. Augusteijn and B. Folkert, "Neural network classification and novelty detection", International Journal on Remote Sensing, Vol.23, No.14, Pp.2891–2902, 2002.

14.   Z. Bakar, R. Mohemad, A. Ahmad and M. Deris, "A comparative study for outlier detection techniques in data mining", Cybernetics and Intelligent Systems IEEE Conference, 2006.

15. D. Barbara and P. Chen, "Using the fractal dimension to cluster datasets", Proc. ACM KDD, Pp.260-264, 2000.

16. D. Barbara, J. Couto, S. Jajodia and N. Wu, "Adam: a tested for exploring the use of data mining in intrusion detection", SIGMOD 4, Pp.15-24, 2001.

17. V. Barnett and T. Lewis, "Outliers in Statistical Data", Wiley, New York, 1994.

18. P. Barson, N. Davey, S.D.H. Field, R.J. Frank and G. McAskie, "The detection of fraud in mobile phone networks", Neural Network World, Vol.6, No.4, 1996.

19. S.D. Bay and M. Schwabacher, "Mining distance-based outliers in near linear time with randomization and a simple pruning rule", 9th ACM SIGKDD Int. Conf. on Knowledge Discovery on Data Mining, 2003.

20. M.J.A. Berry and G.S. Linoff, "Data Mining Techniques For Marketing, Sales And Relationship Management", 2nd Edn., John Wiley, New York, 2004.

21. N. Bhatia, "Survey of Nearest Neighbor Techniques", International Journal of Computer Science and Information Security, Vol. 8, No. 2, 2010.

22. C. Bishop, "Novelty detection and neural network validation", Proceedings of IEEE Vision, Image and Signal Processing, Vol.141, Pp.217-222, 1994.

23. R. Blender, K. Fraedrich and F. Lunkeit, "Identification of cyclone-track regimes in the North Atlantic", Journal of the Royal Meteorological Society, Vol.123, No.539, Pp.727–741, 1997.

24. R.J. Bolton and D.J. Hand, "Statistical fraud detection: A review with discussion", Statistical Science, Vol.17, No.3, Pp. 235-255, 2002.

25. R. Brause, T. Langsdorf and M. Hepp, "Neural data mining for credit card fraud detection", Proceedings of IEEE Artificial Intelligence, Pp.103–106, 1999.

26. M. Breunig, H. Kriegel, R. Ng and J. Sander, "LOF: Identifying density based local outliers", Proc. SIGMOD Conf, Pp.93–104, 2000.

27. P.L. Brockett, X. Xia and R.A.Derrig, "Using Kohonen's self-organizing feature map to uncover automobile bodily injury claims fraud", Journal of Risk and Insurance, 1998.

28. A. Bronstein, J. Das, M. Duro, R. Friedrich, G. Kleyner, M. Mueller, S. Singhal and I. Cohen, "Bayesian networks for detecting anomalies in internet based services", Integrated Network Management, 2001.

29. S.D. Byers and A.E. Raftery, "Nearest neighbor cluster removal for estimating features in spatial point processes", Journal of the American Statistical Association, Vol.93, Pp.577–584, 1998.

30. C. Campbell and K. Bennett, "A linear programming approach to novelty detection", Proceedings of Advances in Neural Information Processing, Vol.14, Pp.55-60, 2000.

31. S. Chakraborty and N.K. Nagwani, "Analysis and Study of Incremental DBSCAN Clustering Algorithm", International Journal of Enterprise Computing And Business Systems, Vol. 1, 2011.

32. V. Chatzigiannakis, S. Papavassiliou, M. Grammatikou and B. Maglaris, "Hierarchical outlier detection in distributed large-scale sensor networks", IEEE on Computers and Communications, Pp.761–767, 2006.

33. Chen Ning, Chen An and Zhou Longxiang, "An Incremental grid Density Based Clustering Algorithm", Journal of Software, Vol.13, No.1, Pp.1-7, 2002.

34. D. Chen, X. Shao, B. Hu and Q. Su, "Simultaneous wavelength selection and outlier detection in multivariate regression of near-infrared spectra", Analytical Sciences, Vol.21, No.2, Pp.161–167, 2005.

35. M.S. Chen, J. Han and P.S. Yu, "Data mining: An overview from a database Perspective", IEEE Trans. Knowledge and Data Engineering, Vol.8, Pp.866-883, 1996.

36. C.C. Hwang, A. Fu and J. Han, "Efficient Rule-Based Attributed-Oriented Induction For Data Mining", Journal Of Intelligent Information Systems, Vol.15, No.21, Pp.175-200, 2000.

37. C. Chow and D.Y. Yeung, "Parzen-window network intrusion detectors", Proceedings of Pattern Recognition. IEEE Computer Society, Vol. 4, 2002.

38. K.C. Cox, S.G. Eick, G.J. Wills and R.J. Brachman, "Visual data mining: Recognizing telephone calling fraud", Journal of Data Mining and Knowledge Discovery, Vol.1, No.2, Pp.225–231, 1997.

39. D. Dasgupta and F. Nino, "A comparison of negative and positive selection algorithms in novel pattern detection", IEEE Cybernetics, Vol.1, Pp.125 -130, 2000.

40. M. Davy and S. Godsill, "Detection of abrupt spectral changes using support vector machines, An application to audio signal segmentation", IEEE Signal Processing. Orlando, 2002.

41. Deepti Sisodia, Lokesh Singh, Sheetal Sisodia and Khushboo saxena, "Clustering Techniques: A Brief Survey of Different Clustering Algorithms", International Journal of Latest Trends in Engineering and Technology, Vol.1, No.3, Pp.82-87, 2012.

42. R. Delmater and M. Hancock, "Data Mining Explained: A Managers Guide To Customer-Centric Business Intelligence", Digital Press, Boston, 2002.

43.   D.E. Denning, "An intrusion detection model", IEEE Transactions of Software Engineering, Vol.13, No.2, Pp.222–232, 1987.

44.   Derya Birant and Alp Kut, "ST-DBSCAN: An Algorithm for Clustering Spatial-temporal data", Data and Knowledge Engineering, Pp.208-221, 2007.

45.   M. Desforges, P. Jacob and J. Cooper, "Applications of probability density estimation to the detection of abnormal conditions in engineering", Proceedings of Institute of Mechanical Engineers, Vol.212, Pp.687-703, 1998.

46.   C. Diehl and J. Hampshire, "Real-time object classification and novelty detection for collaborative video surveillance", IEEE on Neural Networks, 2007.

47.   Domenica Arlia and Massimo Coppola, "Experiments in Parallel Clustering with DBSCAN", 2001.

48.   S. Donoho, "Early detection of insider trading in option markets", Proceedings of the ACM SIGKDD on Knowledge discovery and data mining, Pp.420–429, 2004.

49.   J.R. Dorronsoro, F. Ginel, C. Sanchez and C.S. Cruz, "Neural fraud detection in credit card operations", IEEE Transactions On Neural Networks, Vol.8, No.4, Pp.827 -834, 1997.

50.   W. Du, L. Fang and Peng N. Lad, "localization outlier detection for wireless sensor networks", J. Parallel Distrib. Comput., Vol.66, No.7, Pp.874-886, 2006.

51.   L. Duan, L. Xu, F. Guo, J. Lee and B. Yan, "A local-density based spatial clustering algorithm with noise", Information systems, Vol.32, No.7, Pp.978-986, 2007.

52.   V. Emamian, M. Kaveh and A.Tewfik, "Robust clustering of acoustic emission signals using the Kohonen", IJCSI International Journal of Computer Science, Vol.9, 2012.

53.   E. Eskin, A. Arnold, M. Prerau, L. Portnoy and S. Stolfo, "A geometric framework for unsupervised anomaly detection: Detecting intrusions in unlabeled data", Data Mining for Security Applications, 2002.

54.   M. Ester, H.P. Kriegel, J. Sander and X. Xu, "A density-based algorithm for discovering clusters in large spatial databases with noise", Proceedings of the 2nd International Conference on Knowledge Discovery and Data Mining, Pp.226–231, 1996.

55.   T. Fawcett and F. Provost, "Activity monitoring: noticing interesting changes in behavior",Proceedings of the ACM SIGKDD on Knowledge Discovery and Data Mining, Pp.53-62. 1999.

56.   U.M. Fayyad, G. Piatetsky, P. Shapiro, Smyth and R. Uthurusamy, "Advances in Knowledge Discovery and Data Mining", AAAI/MIT Press, 1996.

57.   U.M. Fayyad, G. Grinstein and A. Wierse, "Information Visualization in Data Mining and Knowledge Discovery", Morgan Kaufmann, Harcourt Intl., 2001.

58.   O. Folorunso and A.O. Ogunde, "Data Mining As A Technique For Knowledge Management In Business Process Redesign", The Electronic Journal Of Knowledge Management, Vol.2, No.1, Pp.33-44, 2004.

59.   S. Forrest, P. D'haeseleer and P. Helman, "An immunological approach to change detection: Algorithms, analysis and implications", IEEE Computer Society, Vol.110, 1996.

60.   S. Forrest, C. Warrender and B. Pearlmutter, "Detecting intrusions using system calls: Alternate data models", IEEE Computer Society, Pp.133–145, 1999.

61.   S. Forrest, F. Esponda and P. Helman, "A formal framework for positive and negative detection schemes", IEEE Transactions on Systems, Man and Cybernetics, Pp.357–373, 2004.

62.   S. Forrest, A.S. Perelson, L. Allen and R. Cherukuri, "Self non self discrimination in a computer", IJCSI International Journal of Computer Science Issues, Vol.9, No.3, 2012.

63.   W.J. Frawley, G. Piatetsky-Shapiro and C.J. Matheus, "Knowledge Discovery in Databases: An Overview", AAAI/MIT Press, 1991.

64.   R. Fujimaki, T. Yairi and K. Machida, "An approach to spacecraft outlier detection problem using kernel feature space", ACM Knowledge discovery in data mining, Pp.401–410, 2005.

65.   G.Y. Xia, "A grid-based density-confidence-interval clustering algorithm for multi-density dataset in large spatial database", International Conference on Intelligent Systems Design and Applications, Vol.1, Pp.713–717, 2006.

66.   A.K. Ghosh, J. Wanken and F. Charron, "Detecting anomalous and unknown intrusions against programs", Proceedings of the IEEE Computer Society, 1998.

67.   S. Ghosh and D.L. Reilly, "Credit card fraud detection with a neural-network", Proceedings IJCSI International Journal of Computer Science Issues, Vol.9, No3, 2012.

68.   G.H. Shah, C.K. Bhensdadia and A.P. Ganatra, "An Empirical Evaluation of density based clustering technique", International Journal of Soft Computing and Engineering, Vol.2, No.1, 2012.

69.   P.S. Goldschmidt, "Compliance Monitoring For Anomaly Detection", Patent No. US 6983266 B1, 2006.

70.   R. Gwadera, M.J. Atallah and W. Szpankowski, "Reliable detection of episodes in event sequences", Knowledge and Information Systems, Vol.7, No.4, Pp.415-437, 2005.

71. A.S. Hadi, "Identifying multiple outliers in multivariate data", Journal of the Royal Statistical Society, Series B, Vol.54, Pp.761-771, 1992.

72. A.S. Hadi, "A modification of a method for the detection of outliers in multivariate samples", Journal of the Royal Statistical Society, Series B, Vol.56, No.2, 1994.

73. A.S. Hadi, A.H.M.R. Imon and M. Werner, "Detection of outliers", Computational Statistics, Vol. 1, Pp.57-70, 2009.

74. J. Han and M. Kamber, "Data mining: concepts and techniques", 2001.

75. D. Hand, H. Mannila and P. Smith, "Principles of Data Mining", MIT Press, Cambridge: MA, 2001.

76. D. Hawkins, "Identification of Outliers", Chapman and Hall, 1980.

77. He Zengyou, Xu Xiaofei, Deng Shengchun and Squeezer, "An efficient algorithm for clustering categorical data", Journal of Computer Science and Technology, Pp.611-624, 2002.

78. Z. He, X. Xu and S. Deng, "Discovering Cluster-based local outliers", Pattern Recognition Pp.1641–1650, 2003.

79. A. Hinneburg and D.A. Keim, "An efficient approach to clustering in large multimedia databases with noise", Proceedings of the 4th International Conference on Knowledge Discovery and Data Mining, Pp.58–65, 1998,

80. A. Hinneburg and D.A. Keim, "A general approach to clustering in large databases with noise", Knowledge and Information Systems (KAIS), Vol.5, No.4, Pp.387-415, 2003.

81. S.A. Hofmeyr, S. Forrest and A. Somayaji, "Intrusion detection using sequences of system calls", Journal of Computer Security, Vol.6, No.3, Pp.151–180, 1998.

82. J. Hsu "Data Mining Trends And Developments: The Key Data Mining Technologies And Applications For The 21st Century", Available At Citeseerx.Ist.Psu.Edu/Viewdoc.

83. Z. Huang, "Extensions to the k-Means Algorithm for Clustering Large Dataset with Categorical Values", Data Mining and Knowledge Discovery, Vol.2, Pp.283–304, 1998.

84. J. Huysmans, B. Baesens, D. Martens, K. Denys and J. Vanthienen, "New trends in data mining", Tijdschrift voor economie en Management, Vol.50, No.4, Pp.697-711, 2005.

85. T. Ide and H. Kashima, "Eigenspace-based outlier detection in computer systems", ACM on Knowledge discovery and data mining, Pp.440–449, 2004.

86. A. Ihler, J. Hutchins and P. Smyth "Adaptive event detection with time-varying Poisson processes", ACM on Knowledge discovery and data mining, Pp.207–216, 2006.

87. A.K. Jain, M.N. Murty and P.J. Flyn, "Data Clustering: A Review", ACM Computing Surveys, Vol.31, No.3, 1999.

88.   S. Jakubek and T. Strasser, "Fault-diagnosis using neural networks with ellipsoidal basis functions", Proceedings of the neural network, Vol.5, Pp.3846-3851, 2002.

89.   D. Jensen, "Data Snooping, Dredging And Fishing: The Dark Side Of Data Mining", SIGKDD Explorations, Vol.1, No.2, Pp. 52-54, 2000.

90.   Jianhao Tan and Jing Zhang, "An Improved Clustering Algorithm Based on Density Distribution Function", Computer and Information Science, Vol.3, No.3, 2010.

91.   W. Jin, A. Tung and J. Han, "Mining top-n local outliers in large databases" Proceedings of the 7th International Conference on Knowledge Discovery and Data-mining, 2001.

92.   Ji Zhan, "Advancement of outlier detection: survey", ICST Transaction on scalable information systems, 2013.

93.   M. Kantardzic, "Data Mining: Concepts, Models, Methods And Algorithms", John Wiley; New Jersey, 2003.

94.   H. Kargupta, "Collective Data Mining", Advances In Distributed Data Mining, Karhgupta And Chan, Editors, MIT Press, 2000.

95.   H. Kargupta and A. Joshi, "Data Mining To Go: Ubiquitous KDD For Mobile And Distributed Environments", Presentation, KDD 2001.

96.   Kejia Zhang, H.G. Shengfei Shi and J. Li, "Unsupervised outlier detection in sensor networks using aggregation tree", Advanced Data Mining and Applications, Pp.158-169, 2007.

97.   E. Keogh, S. Lonardi and B.Y. Chi' Chiu, "Finding surprising patterns in a time series database in linear time and space", Proceedings of the ACM SIGKDD on Knowledge discovery and data mining, Pp.550–556, 2002.

98.   E. Keogh, J. Lin, S.H. Lee and H.V. Herle, "Finding the most unusual time series subsequence: algorithms and applications", Journal of Knowledge and Information Systems, Vol.11, No.1, Pp.1–27, 2006.

99.   S.P. King, D.M. King, K. Astley, L. Tarassenko, P. Hayton and S. Utete, "The use of novelty detection techniques for monitoring high-integrity plant", Proceedings of the International Conference on Control Applications, Vol.1, Pp.221-226, 2002.

100.   W. Klosgen and J.M. Zytkow, "Handbook Of Data Mining And Knowledge Discovery", OUP; Oxford, 2002.

101.   K.M. Knorr and R.T. Ng, "Algorithms for mining distance-based outliers in large datasets", Proc. of the 24rd Int. Conf. on Very Large Data Bases, Pp. 392-403, 1998.

102. K.M. Knorr, R. Ng and V. Tucakov "Distance-based outliers: Algorithms and applications", The International Journal on Very Large Data Bases Journal, Vol.8, Pp.237–253, 2000.

103. C. Kruegel and G. Vigna, "Anomaly detection of web-based attacks", Proceedings of the 10th ACM conference on Computer and communications security, ACM Press, Pp.251-261, 2003.

104. C. Kruegel, D. Mutz, W. Robertson and F. Valeur , "Bayesian event classification for intrusion detection", Proceedings of the IEEE Computer Security Applications, 2003.

105. V. Kumar, "An Empirical Study of the Applications of Data Mining Techniques in Higher Education", International Journal of Advanced Computer Science and Applications, Vol.2, No.3, Pp.80-84, 2011.

106. V. Kumar, "Data Mining for Network Intrusion Detection", NSF Workshop on Next Generation Data Mining, 2002.

107. J. Laurikkala, M. Juhola and E. Kentala, "Informal Identification of Outliers in Medical Data", Fifth International Workshop on Intelligent Data Analysis in Medicine and Pharmacology IDAMAP-2000 Berlin, Organized as a workshop of the 14th European Conference on Artificial Intelligence ECAI-2000.

108. S. Langdell, Use Of "Data Mining In Financial Applications", Data Analysis And Visualization Group At NAG Ltd

109. D.T. Larose, "Discovering Knowledge In Data: An Introduction To Data Mining", John Wiley; New York, 2005.

110. X. Li, J. Han, S. Kim and H. Gonzalez, "Roam: Rule-and motif-based anomaly detection in massive moving object data sets", Proceedings of 7th SIAM International Conference on Data Mining, 2007.

111. J. Lin, E. Keogh, A. Fu and H.V. Herle, "Approximations to magic: Finding unusual medical time series", Proceedings of the 18th IEEE on Computer-Based Medical Systems, Pp.329–334, 2005.

112. C. Lu, D. Chen and Y. Kou, "Algorithms for spatial outlier detection", Proceedings of the 3rd IEEE International Conference on Data-mining, 2003.

113. M.E. Alzaalan, R.T. Aldahdooh and W. Ashour, "EOPTICS "Enhancement Ordering Points to Identify the Clustering Structure", International Journal of Computer Applications, Vol.40, No.17, Pp.1-6, 2012.

114. C. Manikopoulos and S.Papavassiliou, "Network intrusion and fault detection: A statistical outlier approach", IEEE Communication, Vol.40, 2002.

115. G. Manson, S.G. Pierce, K. Worden, T. Monnier, P. Guy and K. Atherton, "Long- term stability of normal condition data for novelty detection", Smart Structures and Integrated Systems, Pp.323-334, 2000.

116. M. Markou and S. Singh, "Novelty detection: a review-part 2: neural network based approaches", Signal Processing, Vol.83, No.12, Pp.2499-2521, 2003.

117. Martin Ester, Han-peter Kriegel, Jorg Sander and Xiaowei Xu, "A Density-Based Algorithm for Discovering Clusters in Large Spatial Databases with Noise", 2nd International conference on Knowledge Discovery and Data Mining, 1996.

118. Miller and J. Han (eds.), "Geographic Data Mining and Knowledge Discovery", Taylor and Francis, 2001.

119. A.T. Murray and V. Estivill-Castro, "Cluster discovery techniques for exploratory spatial data analysis", International Journal of Geographical Information Science, Vol.12, No. 5, Pp.431-443, 1998.

120. A. Nairac, T. Corbett-Clark, R. Ripley, N. Townsend and L. Tarassenko, "Choosing an appropriate model for novelty detection", IEEE on Artificial Neural Networks, Pp.227-232, 1997.

121. R.T. Ng and J. Han, "Efficient and effective cluster methods for spatial data mining", Proc. 20th Int. Conf. on Very Large Data Bases. Santiago, Chile, Pp.144–155, 1994.

122. C.C. Noble and D.J. Cook, "Graph-based outlier detection", Proceedings of the 9th ACM SIGKDD international conference on Knowledge discovery and data mining, 2003.

123. S. Papadimitriou, LOCI: "Fast outlier detection using the local correlation integral in Proc". of the Int. Conf. on Data Engineering, Pp.315-326, 2003.

124. M. Parimala, D. Lopez and N.C. Senthilkumar, "A Survey on Density Based Clustering Algorithms for Mining Large Spatial Databases", International Journal of Advanced Science and Technology, Vol. 31, 2011.

125. L. Parra, G. Deco and S. Miesbach, "Statistical independence and novelty detection with information preserving nonlinear maps", Journal of Neural Computing, Pp.260–269, 1996.

126. A. Patcha and J.M. Park, "An overview of outlier detection techniques: Existing solutions and latest technological trends", Computer Networks, Vol.51, No.12, Pp.3448-3470, 2007.

127. Peng Yang and Biao Huang, "KNN Based Outlier Detection Algorithm in Large Dataset", International Workshop on Education Technology and Training, Pp 611–613, 2008.

128.   K.I. Penny and I.T. Jolliffe, "A comparison of multivariate outlier detection methods for clinical laboratory safety data", The Statistician, Vol.50, No.3, Pp.295-308, 2001.

129.   H. Peter and A. Antonysamy, "An optimized Density based Clustering Algorithm", International Journal of Computer Applications, Vol.6, 2010.

130.   M.I. Petroveskiy, "Outlier detection algorithms in data mining system", Programming and Computer Software, Vol.29, No.4, Pp.228-237, 2003.

131.   D. Pokrajac, A. Lazarevic and L.J. Latecki, "Incremental local outlier detection for data streams", IEEE on Computational Intelligence and Data Mining, 2007.

132.   Pooja Bata Nagpal and Priyanka Ahlawat Mann "Comparative study of density based clustering algorithm", International Journal of Computer Application, Vol.27, 2011.

133.   D. Pyle, "Business Modeling and Data Mining", Morgan Kaufmann, San Francisco, 2003.

134.   Rajendra Pamula, Jatindra kumar Deka and Sukumar Nandi, "An Outlier Detection Method based on Clustering", Second International Conference on Emerging Applications of information Technology, Pp.253-256, 2011.

135.   R.S. Jalal, A.S. Jalal and M. Kumar, "A Density based Algorithm for Discovering Density varied clusters in Large Spatial Databases", International Journal of Computer Applications, Vol. 3, 2010.

136.   S. Ramaswamy, R. Rastogi and K. Shim, "Efficient algorithms for mining outliers from large data sets", SIGMOD Rec., Vol.29, No.2, Pp.427-438, 2000.

137.   S. Roberts, "Novelty detection using extreme value statistics", Proceedings of IEEE - Vision, Image and Signal processing, Pp.124-129, 1999.

138.   R. Das, D.K. Bhattacharyya and J.K. Kalita, "A Frequent Itemset-Nearest Neighbor Based Approach for Clustering Gene Expression Data", Proceedings of Fifth Biotechnology and Bioinformatics Symposium, Pp.73-78, 2008.

139.   P. Rousseeuw and A. Leory, "Robust Regression and Outlier Detection", Wiley Series in Probability and Statistics, 1987.

140.   S. Roy and D.K Bhattacharyya, "An approach to find embedded clusters using density based techniques", Proceedings of the ICDCIT, Lecture Notes in Computer Science, Vol.3816, Pp.523–535, 2005.

141.   S. Goele and N. Chanana, "Data Mining Trend In Past, Current And Future", International Journal of Computing & Business Research, 2012.

142.   J. Sander, M. Ester, H.P. Kriegel and X. Xu, "Density-based clustering in spatial databases: The algorithm GDBSCAN and its applications", Data Mining and Knowledge Discovery, Pp.169-194, 1997.

143. Santosh Kumar Rai, Nishchol Mishra "DBCSVM: Density Based Clustering Using Support Vector Machines", IJCSI International Journal of Computer Science Issues, Vol. 9, No. 2, Pp. 223-230, 2012.

144. R. Sekar, M. Bendre, D. Dhurjati and P. Bollineni, "A fast automation-based method for detecting anomalous program behaviors", Proceedings of the IEEE Symposium on Security and Privacy, IEEE Computer Society, 144, 2001.

145. S. Shekhar, C.T. Lu and P. Zhang, "Detecting Graph-Based Spatial Outlier: Algorithms and Applications (A Summary of Results)", Proc. of the Seventh ACM-SIGKDD Conference on Knowledge Discovery and Data Mining, SF, CA, 2001.

146. S. Shekhar, C.T. Lu and P. Zhang, "Detecting Graph-Based Spatial Outlier", Intelligent Data Analysis: An International Journal, Vol.6, No.5, Pp.451–468, 2002.

147. C. Siaterlis and B. Maglaris, "Towards multisensor data fusion for DoS detection", Proceedings of the ACM on Applied computing, Pp.439-446, 2004.

148. S. Singh and M. Markou, "An approach to novelty detection applied to the classification of image regions", IEEE Trans. on Knowledge and Data Engineering, Pp.396-407, 2009.

149. R. Smith, A. Bivens, M. Embrechts, C. Palagiri and B. Szymanski, "Clustering approaches for outlier based intrusion detection", Proceedings of Intelligent Engineering Systems through Artificial Neural Networks, 2002.

150. H. Sohn, K. Worden and C. Farrar, "Novelty detection under changing environmental conditions", SPIE 2001.

151. H.E. Solberg and A. Lahti, "Detection of outliers in reference distributions: Performance of Horn's algorithm", Clinical Chemistry, 2005.

152. X. Song, M. Wu, C. Jermaine and S. Ranka, "Conditional outlier detection", IEEE Transactions on Knowledge and Data Engineering, Vol.19, No.5, Pp.631-645, 2007.

153. Q. Song, W. Hu and W. Xie, "Robust support vector machine with bullet hole image classification", IEEE Trans. on Systems, Man, and Cybernetics, Vol.32, No.4, 2002.

154. C. Spence, L. Parra and P. Sajda, "Detection, synthesis and compression in mammographic image analysis with a hierarchical image probability model", Computer Society, 2001.

155. Stefan Brecheisen, Hans-Peter Kriegel and Martin Pfeifle "Efficient Density-Based Clustering of Complex Objects", Proc. 4th IEEE International Conference on Data Mining, Pp.43-50, 2004.

156. I. Steinwart, D. Hush and C. Scovel, "A classification framework for outlier detection", Journal of Machine Learning Research, Vol.6, Pp.211–232, 2005.

157.   J. Sun, H. Qu, D. Chakrabarti and C. Faloutsos, "Neighborhood formation and outlier detection in bipartite graphs", IEEE on Data Mining, Pp.418-425, 2009.

158.   P. Sun, S. Chawla and B. Arunasalam, "Mining for outliers in sequential databases", IJCSI International Journal of Computer Science Issues, Vol. 9, No.3, 2012.

159.   C. Surace, K. Worden and G. Tomlinson, "A novelty detection approach to diagnose damage in a cracked beam", SPIE, Vol. 3089, Pp.947-953, 1997.

160.   E. Suzuki, T. Watanabe, H. Yokoi and K. Takabayashi, "Detecting interesting exceptions from medical test data with visual summarization", Proceedings of the IEEE on Data Mining, Pp. 315–322, 2003.

161.   H. Teng, K. Chen and S.Lu, "Adaptive real-time outlier detection using inductively generated sequential patterns", IJCSI International Journal of Computer Science, Vol.9, No. 3, 2012.

162.   J. Theiler and D.M. Cai, "Re-sampling approach for outlier detection in multispectral images", SPIE, Pp.230-240, 2003.

163.   B.T. Thuraisingham, "Security issues for data warehousing and data mining", Database Security X: Status and Prospects, Proceedings of the Tenth International Conference on Database Security, 1997.

164.   M. Vijayalakshmi and M. Renuka Devi, "A Survey of Different Issue of Different clustering Algorithms Used in Large Data sets", International Journal of Advanced Research in Computer Science and Software Engineering, Pp.305-307, 2012.

165.   G.J. Willams, R. A. Baster, H. He, S. Harkins and L. Gu, "A comparative study of RNN for outlier detection in data mining", Proceedings of ICDM, Pp.709-712, 2002.

166.   K. Yamanishi and J. Ichi Takeuchi, "Discovering outlier filtering rules from unlabeled data: combining a supervised learner with an unsupervised learner", ACM on Knowledge discovery and data mining, Pp.389-394, 2001.

167.   Y.M. Cheung, "k*-Means: A new generalized k-means clustering algorithm", Pattern Recognition Letters, Vol.24, Pp.2883–2893, 2003.

168.   S. Zhou, Y. Zhao, J. Guan & Z. Huang, "A neighborhood-based clustering algorithm", Ninth Pacific-Asia Conference on Knowledge Discovery and Data Mining, Pp.361–371, 2005.

169.   Zhou Yonggeng, Zhou Aoying and Cao Jing, "DBSCAN Algorithm Based Data Partition", Journal of Computer Research and Development, Vol.37, No.10, Pp.1153-1159, 2000.

170.   S. Zhou, A. Zhou et. al, "A Fast Density-Based Clustering Algorithm", Journal of Computer Research and Development, Vol.37, No.11, Pp.1287-1292, 2003.

www.ingramcontent.com/pod-product-compliance
Lightning Source LLC
Chambersburg PA
CBHW050524160726
48003CB00001B/442